William Strunk, Jr.

THE ELEMENTS OF
STYLE

UPDATED AND ANNOTATED
FOR PRESENT-DAY USE

Stanford Pritchard

SPRINGSIDE BOOKS
MIDDLEBURY, VERMONT
NEW YORK, NEW YORK

For Anthony Bly

TABLE OF CONTENTS

FOREWORD

THE ELEMENTS OF STYLE

§

USAGE

LITTLE DOTS AND SQUIGGLY THINGS

ROGUE'S GALLERY

Foreword

The ancients wrote at a time when the great art
of writing badly had not yet been invented. In those
days to write at all meant to write well.
— Georg Christoph Lichtenberg

Strunk and White....

Rarely in the annals of publishing has a book been known as much by the names of its authors as by its title, but such is the case with *The Elements of Style* by William Strunk, Jr., and E. B. White. This compact guide to simple, clear, and precise writing has become an indispensable reference work, a veritable *vade mecum* (constant companion) for countless numbers of students and professionals, and has sold over ten million copies. Having become a classic, it still sells briskly.

William Strunk, Jr., was a professor of English at Cornell University where, in 1918, he privately published for the use of his students his little —emphasis on *little*: it was only forty-three pages—book of grammatical and stylistic rules. In 1959, one of Strunk's former students, E. B. White, at the time an editor and writer for *The New Yorker*, and the author of *Stuart Little* and *Charlotte's Web*, among others, added to, and revised the book; he revised it again in 1972 and 1979, and subsequent editions appeared in 1999 (with minor revisions made anonymously), and 2005 (with illustrations). The meeting of these two minds, Strunk and White (Strunk died in 1946, White in 1985), proved serendipitous. The book proved enormously popular and, as noted, today is known as much by the names of its authors as by its title.

From time to time people say to me: "Your work is so well *crafted*." At first I took this as a compliment, but eventually I began to think: *no, no, no, my work is* not *well crafted! I simply write according to the rules and procedures I was taught, the rules and procedures whose observation was noteworthy in all the good writers I read!* (I recently read two books and the copy on a record jacket, both from the 1960s, that left me feeling: hell, people don't even understand, anymore, what it is to write like this, they don't see how simply solid, tasteful, and elegant this writing is. I was left with the melancholy feeling that I was visiting a lost world.) It disheartens me to say it, but most of what I read, nowadays, is pedestrian at best, sloppy in the middle, and atrocious at worst. Newspaper and magazine articles are riddled with infelicities and outright grammatical errors, and clichés, buzzwords, and hackneyed expressions are everywhere. I am routinely left pining for that lost world of the Fifties and Sixties, all the while asking myself: what went wrong?

Am I set in my ways? Am I stodgy, an elitist, worse, a snob? I do not believe I am. But when I see a sentence like, "Each person is entitled to their opinion," or "They only sold six tickets to the play," I wince, and my teeth tingle. Such writing has become all too common; that doesn't mean it's not inexcusable. (The only places where I've never seen a single grammatical or typographical error are annual reports, which suggests where the priorities are, in this country.) As music theory is not prescriptive, but comes along after the fact and describes the procedures by which the best composers and improvisers have composed or performed, so grammatical rules trail along after language and describe what, at any given moment, has been thought to be the best grammar and the best usage. Language is always in flux, and times change; I realize that. But language is like a game: It's only fun if we agree to abide by certain pre-established rules. If the rules are going to change, they ought to be made to force their way in, so to speak, they ought to be made to *prove* their usefulness over an extended period of time. A President on vacation may say to those around him, "I ain't played a good game of golf all week," but at present, he or she can't use the word "ain't" in a State of the Union address. That's just the way the game is currently played. ("Ain't," by the way, was once a common, more or less respectable word. But the rules of the game gradually evolved in such a way that it is currently considered inappropriate in proper, especially formal, English.)

Consider this quote from Robert Frost, *apropos* writing free verse: "I had as soon . . . play tennis with the net down." Quite simply, without agreed-upon rules and procedures, the game is not *fun*; all the pleasure comes from seeing how the moves are made, and objectives accomplished, within commonly accepted rules and restrictions. When anything and everything is permitted—when everything is up for grabs—there is no way to determine what is, and is not, proper speech. When a friend of mine says, "I'm going to lay down," I always ask him where he got the down. One *lays* tiles, carpet, or eggs; one *lies* down. Sadly, both in speech and in writing, this particular violation of correct grammar has become so widespread that it threatens to provoke a rule change.

Incidentally, I am aware that the philosopher Ludwig Wittgenstein pioneered a concept of "language-games." His metaphor tended to be more narrow and specific than mine, however. I want merely to encourage American speakers and American writers (and my annotations to Strunk's book are directed *primarily* to Americans) to see that we are all involved in a communal activity, speaking and writing, in which the rules are conducive to pleasure, that far from being onerous, far from being a burden or an imposition, they are precisely what enables us to recognize elegance in speech and writing. The subtlety of their observance is precisely why we consider some writers good, some speakers refined, and others not.

It may be worthwhile to digress, for a moment, and consider the currents that were in the air when William Strunk began his linguistic housecleaning. Everywhere—in literature, music, the visual arts, technology, industrial design—the fresh wind known as Modernism was blowing. In one of its manifestations, Cubism was busy dissecting its subjects and viewing them from multiple angles. Braque, Picasso, and Juan Gris were among those working within this new "collage aesthetic," and through Gertrude Stein (who owned paintings by all three) transmitting it to writers; the influences, of course, were reciprocal. Sherwood Anderson, Thornton Wilder, and Samuel Beckett were among those who were influenced by the new aesthetic; more than anyone else, however, it was Ernest Hemingway who was drawn to the new, lean, pared-down style, and pioneered the flight from the clutter, bric-a-brac, and grandiloquence associated with Victorian style.

In architecture, meanwhile, the notion that "form follows function," popularized by Louis Sullivan, was in ascendancy, and Frank Lloyd Wright had begun designing houses with that principle in mind; at least until the regrettable advent of postmodernist architecture, ornamentation for the sake of ornamentation was shunned by leading architects. Surrealism, Futurism, Constructivism, and Dada had the similar effect of stripping from the plastic arts all that was not functional, not essential. (Marcel Duchamp exhibited one of his "found objects," or "ready-mades," an essentially unadorned urinal, the year before Strunk published his little book.) In music, Erik Satie's *Gymnopédies* had earlier set a standard for simplicity and austerity; Charles Ives's compositions, while not simple (and even when amusing), were *all business*. In philosophy, Pragmatism was still dominant; in industrial design, the tendency had begun to streamline machines and machinery.

Finally, 1918, the year William Strunk privately printed his little book, was the year World War I ended. It would be unreasonable to think that a war that changed forever so many aspects of Western culture didn't also have its effect on language. After the horror of the war, it no longer seemed appropriate to employ euphemisms and superfluous embellishment, no longer appropriate to appeal to flowery, soap-bubble language, above all, no longer appropriate to wallow in easy sentimentality. What was wanted was a language that was clean, spare, efficient, and precise. As effectively as any other person during the postwar period, William Strunk codified that new language.

Now, E.B. White's work is a wonderful amplification of Strunk's "little book" (as it was called on the Cornell campus). It lays down many additional rules and proper usages, and fleshes out the original with two entire new chapters. White's emendations, however, do not contain any critique of the many errors and incorrect usages that have fastened, like cancers, onto current English. Curiously, furthermore, White ignores a number of rules set down by his own mentor, and uses phrases like "peculiar stance," and "in the main," that I consider infelicitous at best. ("In the main" always leads me to picture myself *in* one.)

So let us go back to the *urtext*, Strunk's original forty-three pages, allow him a few amplifications from the first commercial edition of his book (1920), and see the way he thinks; as we do so, we'll observe how some of the rules of his day have changed. I propose to be your guide, or at least your companion, during this adventure. Along the way, I will show you how I approach any text I have to edit, including my own manuscripts; my comments are in bold, between brackets. In making these comments, I hope to give a sense of the level of care that is involved, better, the level of care that is *necessary*.

As the American poet, Marianne Moore, said: "There is a great deal of poetry in unconscious fastidiousness."

Let the games begin.

Stanford Pritchard earned a B.A. in philosophy from Haverford College, and on a Rockefeller Fellowship studied at the University of Chicago. He has worked, or written for, *The New York Review of Books*, *The New York Free Press*, and *Cavalier*, and has been published in *The International Philosophical Quarterly*, *Psychoanalysis and Psychotherapy*, *The Kenyon*, *New England*, and *Wisconsin Reviews*, and elsewhere. Pritchard's collection of short stories, *Terminal Vibrato*, is available from Beaufort Books, New York; his novels include *Restaurant, Symphony*, *Benny's Mission*, and *Three Sexes in Search of the Creddlebones*. A generous sampling of his work, and a more complete résumé, may be viewed at stanfordpritchard.com.

THE ELEMENTS OF STYLE

I. Introductory

This book is intended for use in English courses in which the practice of composition is combined with the study of literature. It aims to give in brief space the principal requirements of plain English style. It aims to lighten the task of instructor and student by concentrating attention (in Chapters II and III) on a few essentials, the rules of usage and principles of composition most commonly violated. The numbers of the sections may be used as references in correcting manuscript.

["...plain English style." It is worth pausing over this seemingly innocuous phrase. "Plain Style" (it is often capitalized), also known as "Plain English," was premeditatedly designed to be a language that eschews jargon, technical terms, slang, vulgar phrases, foreign idioms, and long and ambiguous sentences. Plain Style does not allow pedantry, affectation, or excessive embellishment. Although its influences go back to the classical period, Plain Style may be said to have originated in the scientific, poetic, and religious writing of the seventeenth century. Strunk's little book was a major influence in the adoption of Plain Style in the twentieth century—a style, which, at its best, is as simply elegant, and beautifully functional, as Shaker furniture.

English, when written and spoken properly, is a very *efficient* language. When signs are posted, or instructions given, in several languages, one of them being English, it is almost always the English that requires the fewest syllables. As an extreme contrast, Arabic (at least as spoken) tends to be extremely flowery and ornate; even the act of saying "good morning" can easily blossom into poetry.]

The book covers only a small portion of the field of English style, but the experience of its writer has been that once past the essentials, students profit most by individual instruction based on the problems of their own work, and that each instructor has his own body of theory, which he prefers to that offered by any textbook.

The writer's colleagues in the Department of English in Cornell University have greatly helped him in the preparation of his manuscript. Mr. George McLane Wood has kindly consented to the inclusion under Rule 11 of some material from his *Suggestions to Authors.*

The following books are recommended for reference or further study: in connection with Chapters II and IV, F. Howard Collins, *Author and Printer* (Henry Frowde); Chicago University Press, *Manual of Style;* T. L. De Vinne *Correct Composition* (The Century Company); Horace Hart, *Rules for Compositors and Printers* (Oxford University Press); George McLane Wood, *Extracts from the Style-Book of the Government Printing Office* (United States Geological Survey); in connection with Chapters III and V, Sir Arthur Quiller-Couch, *The Art of Writing* (Putnams), especially the chapter, Interlude on Jargon; George McLane Wood, *Suggestions to Authors* (United States Geological Survey); John Leslie Hall, *English Usage* (Scott, Foresman and Co.); James P. Kelly, *Workmanship in Words* (Little, Brown and Co.).

[Most of these books are out of print.]

It is an old observation that the best writers sometimes disregard the rules of rhetoric. When they do so, however, the reader will usually find in the sentence some compensating merit, attained at the cost of the violation. Unless he is certain of doing as well, he will probably do best to follow the rules. After he has learned, by their guidance, to write plain English adequate for everyday uses, let him look, for the secrets of style, to the study of the masters of literature.

II. Elementary Rules of Usage

1. Form the possessive singular of nouns with 's.

Follow this rule whatever the final consonant. Thus write,

> Charles's friend
> Burns's poems
> the witch's malice

This is the usage of the United States Government Printing Office and of the Oxford University Press.

[The second *s* can be omitted after the names of iconic figures of the past: *Jesus', Moses', Confucius', Socrates'*, and after other classical names: *Tacitus', Euripides', Suetonius', Eros'*. A second *s* can also be omitted after plural nouns (*sailors', friends'*), but not after singular ones (*boss's, bus's*). The Style Manual of the United States Government Printing Office has been in use since 1894; though mainly a guide for printers, it is also a testament to the way style and usage change. It is now in its thirtieth edition.]

Exceptions are the possessives of ancient proper names in *-es* and *-is*, the possessive *Jesus'*, and such forms as *for conscience' sake, for righteousness' sake*. But such forms as *Achilles' heel, Moses' laws, Isis' temple* are commonly replaced by

> the heel of Achilles
> the laws of Moses
> the temple of Isis

[The annotator prefers *conscience's*, the title of Thomas Hardy's story (alluded to) notwithstanding. *Achilles' heel* is a traditional and popular usage, and perfectly acceptable.]

The pronominal possessives *hers, its, theirs, yours*, and *oneself* have no apostrophe.

2. In a series of three or more terms with a single conjunction, use a comma after each term except the last.

Thus write,

> red, white, and blue
> honest, energetic, but headstrong
> He opened the letter, read it, and made a note of its contents.

[This is called the *serial comma*, and using it without exception is an effortless way of promoting order and clarity. It's a crying shame that most magazines and newspapers (where ease of comprehension would seem to be a major objective), as well as many books, forgo it. Without it, some sentences become ambiguous to the point of amusement, e.g., "I had dinner with my parents, Joe Biden and Lady Gaga." (See "comma" in "Little Dots and Squiggly Things," at the end of Usage.)]

This is also the usage of the Government Printing Office and of the Oxford University Press.

In the names of business firms the last comma is omitted, as

> Brown, Shipley and Company

The abbreviation *etc.*, even if only a single term comes before it, is always preceded by a comma.

[And, as noted below, *followed* by a comma, except at the end of a sentence.]

3. Enclose parenthetic expressions between commas.

> The best way to see a country,
> unless you are pressed for time, is to travel on foot.

This rule is difficult to apply; it is frequently hard to decide whether a single word, such as *however*, or a brief phrase, is or is not parenthetic. If the interruption to the flow of the sentence is but slight, the writer may safely omit the commas. But whether the interruption be slight or considerable, he must never omit one comma and leave the other. Such punctuation as:

Marjorie's husband, Colonel Nelson paid us a visit yesterday,
My brother you will be pleased to hear, is now in perfect health,

is indefensible.

[In the paragraph above, note the correct use of the subjunctive, which is a verb tense used for situations that are hypothetical and might or might not exist in fact: "*whether* the interruption *be* slight or...." See "subjunctive, the" in Usage. In the last two examples, Strunk is saying that there need to be commas after *Nelson* and *brother*.]

Non-restrictive relative clauses are, in accordance with this rule, set off by commas.

[Here Strunk needlessly splits up the verb ("clauses *are*, in accordance with this rule, *set off*"), an infelicitous practice that is spreading like a plague. See "Let's-Chop-the-Sentence-Up" in the Rogue's Gallery.]

The audience, which had at first been indifferent,
became more and more interested.

Similar clauses introduced by *where* and *when* are similarly punctuated.

In 1769, when Napoleon was born,
Corsica had but recently been acquired by France.

Nether Stowey, where Coleridge wrote
The Rime of the Ancient Mariner, is a few miles from Bridgewater.

[The title of Coleridge's poem: italicize or put in quotation marks? See "Quotation Marks with Other Punctuation" in Usage.]

In these sentences the clauses introduced by *which*, *when*, and *where* are non-restrictive; they do not limit the application of the words on which they depend, but add, parenthetically, statements supplementing those in the principal clauses. Each sentence is a combination of two statements which might have been made independently.

The audience was at first indifferent.
Later it became more and more interested.

Napoleon was born in 1769. At that time
Corsica had but recently been acquired by France.

Coleridge wrote *The Rime of the Ancient Mariner* at
Nether Stowey. Nether Stowey is only a few miles from Bridgewater.

[Previous page: Tastes change. We would now write "two statements *that* **might have...." The British cleave to** *which*.**]**

Restrictive relative clauses are not set off by commas.

The candidate who best meets these requirements
will obtain the place.

In this sentence the relative clause restricts the application of the word *candidate* to a single person. Unlike those above, the sentence cannot be split into two independent statements.

[Nonrestrictive clauses, of course, do require commas: "The candidate, who had every reason to know, nevertheless refused to answer." For more on this important topic, *restrictive* **and** *nonrestrictive clauses*, **see "that / which" in Usage. Note that Strunk inserts a hyphen after** *non*. **The annotator's omission of it is consistent with the way American English has evolved, namely, its tendency to dispense with the hyphen after many words beginning with the prefixes** *pre, co, semi, anti*, **and** *non*. **The British tend to retain the hyphen.** *Place*, **above: job, position, or post.]**

The abbreviations *etc.* and *jr.* are always preceded by a comma, and except at the end of a sentence, followed by one.

[...A nicety which, more and more, is being overlooked. There are those who argue that because *Jr.* **is an intrinsic part of a surname, it need not be preceded by a comma; the annotator still favors it. Note that** *e.g.* **is always preceded** *and* **followed by a comma.]**

Similar in principle to the enclosing of parenthetic expressions between commas is the setting off by commas of phrases or dependent clauses preceding or following the main clause of a sentence. The sentences quoted in this section and under Rules 4, 5, 6, 7, 16, and 18 should afford sufficient guidance.

If a parenthetic expression is preceded by a conjunction, place the first comma before the conjunction, not after it.

> He saw us coming,
> and unaware that we had learned of his treachery,
> greeted us with a smile.

[A matter of taste, and one's ear for rhythm. Here the annotator prefers the comma after *and*, where it better suggests the parallelism of the verbs, *coming* and *greeted*. See "comma" in Punctuation.]

4. Place a comma before *and* or *but* introducing an independent clause.

> The early records of the city have disappeared,
> and the story of its first years can no longer be reconstructed.

> The situation is perilous,
> but there is still one chance of escape.

[Consistent with proper usage, a comma may be inserted any time the reader (indeed, the writer) may need to catch her breath.]

Sentences of this type, isolated from their context, may seem to be in need of rewriting. As they make complete sense when the comma is reached, the second clause has the appearance of an after-thought. Further, *and,* is the least specific of connectives. Used between independent clauses, it indicates only that a relation exists between them without defining that relation. In the example above, the relation is that of cause and result. The two sentences might be rewritten:

> As the early records of the city have disappeared,
> the story of its first years can no longer be reconstructed.

> Although the situation is perilous,
> there is still one chance of escape.

Or the subordinate clauses might be replaced by phrases:

Owing to the disappearance of the early records of the city,
the story of its first years can no longer be reconstructed.

In this perilous situation,
there is still one chance of escape.

But a writer may err by making his sentences too uniformly compact and periodic, and an occasional loose sentence prevents the style from becoming too formal and gives the reader a certain relief. Consequently, loose sentences of the type first quoted are common in easy, unstudied writing. But a writer should be careful not to construct too many of his sentences after this pattern (see Rule 14).

[For thoughts about the word *context* (above), see Usage. *After-thought* is nowadays streamlined to *afterthought*.]

Two-part sentences of which the second member is introduced by *as* (in the sense of *because*), *for*, *or*, *nor*, and *while* (in the sense of *and at the same time*) likewise require a comma before the conjunction.

If a dependent clause, or an introductory phrase requiring to be set off by a comma, precedes the second independent clause, no comma is needed after the conjunction.

[In the following sentence, one could conceivably delete the comma after *promptly*.]

The situation is perilous,
but if we are prepared to act promptly,
there is still one chance of escape.

For two-part sentences connected by an adverb, see the next section.

5. Do not join independent clauses by a comma.

If two or more clauses, grammatically complete and not joined by a conjunction, are to form a single compound sentence, the proper mark of punctuation is a semicolon.

> Stevenson's romances are entertaining;
> they are full of exciting adventures.

> It is nearly half past five;
> we cannot reach town before dark.

It is of course equally correct to write the above as two sentences each, replacing the semicolons by periods.

> Stevenson's romances are entertaining.
> They are full of exciting adventures.

> It is nearly half past five.
> We cannot reach town before dark.

If a conjunction is inserted, the proper mark is a comma (Rule 4).

> Stevenson's romances are entertaining,
> for they are full of exciting adventures.

> It is nearly half past five,
> and we cannot reach town before dark.

Note that if the second clause is preceded by an adverb, such as *accordingly, besides, so, then, therefore,* or *thus*, and not by a conjunction, the semicolon is still required.

> I had never been in the place before;
> so I had difficulty in finding my way about.

[At the time Strunk wrote, the semicolon was often used in this fashion; it is still so used by the British. Nowadays, we would substitute a comma for the semicolon (and eliminate the *in* before *finding*).]

In general, however, it is best, in writing, to avoid using *so* in this manner; there is danger that the writer who uses it at all may use it too often. A simple correction, usually serviceable, is to omit the word *so,* and begin the first clause with *as:*

> As I had never been in the place before,
> I had difficulty in finding my way about.

If the clauses are very short, and are alike in form, a comma is usually permissible:

> Man proposes, God disposes.

> The gate swung apart,
> the bridge fell, the portcullis was drawn up.

6. Do not break sentences in two.

In other words, do not use periods for commas.

> I met them on a Cunard liner several years ago.
> Coming home from Liverpool to New York.

> He was an interesting talker.
> A man who had traveled all over the world,
> and lived in half a dozen countries.

In both these examples, the first period should be replaced by a comma, and the following word begun with a small letter.

It is permissible to make an emphatic word or expression serve the purpose of a sentence and to punctuate it accordingly:

> Again and again he called out. No reply.

The writer must, however, be certain that the emphasis is warranted, and that he will not be suspected of a mere blunder in punctuation.

Rules 3, 4, 5, and 6 cover the most important principles in the punctuation of ordinary sentences; they should be so thoroughly mastered that their application becomes second nature.

7. A participial phrase at the beginning of a sentence must refer to the grammatical subject.

[A *participle* is a form of verb that has the characteristics of, or acts like, both a verb and a noun (*present participle*), or a verb and an adjective (*past participle*); each shares in, or partakes of (i.e., it *participates* in) these qualities. The first always ends in *–ing*, and when it functions in its "noun" sense, is called a *gerund*: "*Hiking* is fun." Typically, the second ends in *-ed* or *-en*, and is coupled with *was, has, have*, or *had*: "George *had* already *eaten*." Exceptions apply to what are called *irregular verbs*: *sung, rung, swum, brought*.]

> Walking slowly down the road,
> he saw a woman accompanied by two children.

The word *walking* refers to the subject of the sentence, not to the woman. If the writer wishes to make it refer to the woman, he must recast the sentence:

> He saw a woman, accompanied by two children,
> walking slowly down the road.

Participial phrases preceded by a conjunction or by a preposition, nouns in apposition, adjectives, and adjective phrases come under the same rule if they begin the sentence.

[*Nouns in apposition* are nouns that are grammatically parallel, and refer to the same thing or person: *my brother the King, my friend Rodney*. In the following paired examples, as throughout this book, it is the second that is to be preferred.]

On arriving in Chicago,
his friends met him at the station.

When he arrived (or, On his arrival) in Chicago,
his friends met him at the station.

A soldier of proved valor,
they entrusted him with the defence of the city.

A soldier of proved valor,
he was entrusted with the defence of the city.

Young and inexperienced,
the task seemed easy to me.

Young and inexperienced,
I thought the task easy.

Without a friend to counsel him,
the temptation proved irresistible.

Without a friend to counsel him,
he found the temptation irresistible.

[In the third example, the annotator would have preferred *Even though I was...*, possibly *Young and inexperienced as I was....* He would also have substituted the more graphic *found* for *thought*. *Defence*: now chiefly British.]

Sentences violating this rule are often ludicrous.

Being in a dilapidated condition,
I was able to buy the house very cheap.

[The issue, in this section, is loose, ambiguous, dangling modifiers, which leave sentences floating, that is, feeling vague and undefined. The final example, above, features a *dangling participle*, which occurs when a word, usually ending in –ing, could refer either to the subject or the object of the sentence. *Traipsing home through the snow, last night, the city was very quiet.* Was the city traipsing through the snow? *Emerging from the forest, a rainbow appeared.* Did the rainbow emerge from the forest? *Walking slowly down the road, he saw a woman....*]

8. Divide words at line-ends, in accordance with their formation and pronunciation.

If there is room at the end of a line for one or more syllables of a word, but not for the whole word, divide the word, unless this involves cutting off only a single letter, or cutting off only two letters of a long word. No hard and fast rule for all words can be laid down. The principles most frequently applicable are:

[Except when absolutely necessary, don't hyphenate before _ly_ or _ed_, and leave them hanging on the next line.]

a. Divide the word according to its formation:

know-ledge (not *knowl-edge*); *Shake-speare* (not *Shakes-peare*); *de-scribe* (not *des-cribe*); *atmo-sphere* (not *atmos-phere*);

[The operative phrase, above, is "no hard and fast rule can be laid down." Hyphenation is a very inexact art, so inexact that different dictionaries hyphenate identical words differently. Sometimes pronunciation (sound) dictates the preferred hyphenation, other times the operative principle is to retain, intact, a familiar root word; elsewhere there are standard guidelines (hyphenate before the suffixes _–ing_ and _-tion_). The British often hyphenate in ways that seem to Americans completely random, the objective being simply to get as many letters on a line as possible. Pursuant to the hyphenate-by-pronunciation guideline, _knowledge_ is now usually hyphenated _knowl-edge_ (we don't pronounce it _no-ledge_), and _atmosphere_, _atmos-phere_. (As does Strunk, I am hyphenating only between syllables where the choice is ambiguous.) In accordance with the guideline, hyphenate-to-retain-the-root-word, we hyphenate _interesting_, _interest-ing_. But the guidelines are murky and imprecise. Do we hyphenate _patriotism_, _patrio-tism_, in accordance with the way we pronounce it, or _patriot-ism_, in order to retain the root? Some dictionaries recommend the former, some the latter. _Dictio-nary_ or _diction-ary_? Again, it depends on the dictionary. _Sentimen-tal_ or _sentiment-al_? Same thing.]

b. Divide "on the vowel":

edi-ble (not *ed-ible*); *propo-sition*; *ordi-nary*; *espe-cial*; *reli-gious*; *oppo-nents*; *regu-lar*; *classi-fi-ca-tion* (three divisions possible); *deco-rative*; *presi-dent*;

c. Divide between double letters, unless they come at the end of the simple form of the word:

Apen-nines; Cincin-nati; refer-ring; but *tell-ing.*

[Again, the guidelines conflict with one another. To retain the root, *class*, in *classi-fi-ca-tion*, above, one would hyphenate after the second *s* (as Strunk presumably does). But hyphenating "between double letters" would dictate *clas-si-fi-cation,* which is the way it's usually hyphenated.]

The treatment of consonants in combination is best shown from examples:

for-tune; *pic-ture*; *presump-tuous*; *illus-tration*; *sub-stan-tial* (either division); *indus-try; instruc-tion*; *sug-ges-tion*; *incen-diary.*

The student will do well to examine the syllable-division in a number of pages of any carefully printed book.

[...But expect inconsistency from one book to the next. Even the rules laid down, on various subjects, in *The Chicago Manual of Style* must be taken with a grain of salt.]

III. Elementary Principles
of Composition

9. Make the paragraph the unit of composition: one paragraph to each topic.

If the subject on which you are writing is of slight extent, or if you intend to treat it very briefly, there may be no need of subdividing it into topics. Thus a brief description, a brief summary of a literary work, a brief account of a single incident, a narrative merely outlining an action, the setting forth of a single idea, any one of these is best written in a single paragraph. After the paragraph has been written, it should be examined to see whether sub-division will not improve it.

Ordinarily, however, a subject requires subdivision into topics, each of which should be made the subject of a paragraph. The object of treating each topic in a paragraph by itself is, of course, to aid the reader. The beginning of each paragraph is a signal to him that a new step in the development of the subject has been reached.

[...*A signal to him*: *he, him* again. You might try changing *him* to *her*, or leaving out the prepositional phrase entirely. (Similarly, below.) On the delicate subject of avoiding the masculine pronoun, see "his, hers / their" in Usage.]

The extent of subdivision will vary with the length of the composition. For example, a short notice of a book or poem might consist of a single paragraph. One slightly longer might consist of two paragraphs:

A. Account of the work.
B. Critical discussion.

A report on a poem, written for a class in literature, might consist of seven paragraphs:

A. Facts of composition and publication.
B. Kind of poem; metrical form.

C. Subject.
D. Treatment of subject.
E. For what chiefly remarkable.
F. Wherein characteristic of the writer.
G. Relationship to other works.

The contents of paragraphs C and D would vary with the poem. Usually, paragraph C would indicate the actual or imagined circumstances of the poem (the situation), if these call for explanation, and would then state the subject and outline its development. If the poem is a narrative in the third person throughout, paragraph C need contain no more than a concise summary of the action. Paragraph D would indicate the leading ideas and show how they are made prominent, or would indicate what points in the narrative are chiefly emphasized.

A novel might be discussed under the heads:

A. Setting.
B. Plot.
C. Characters.
D. Purpose.

A historical event might be discussed under the heads:

A. What led up to the event.
B. Account of the event.
C. What the event led up to.

[It's a minor point, but because *head* has so many meanings, we ought probably to write *headings*. Example C: Note that it's not *always* bad to end a sentence with a preposition; to avoid awkwardness, in fact, it is often necessary.]

In treating either of these last two subjects, the writer would probably find it necessary to subdivide one or more of the topics here given.

[*Topics here given*, or *given topics*.]

As a rule, single sentences should not be written or printed as paragraphs. An exception may be made of sentences of transition, indicating the relation between the parts of an exposition or argument.

[Previous page: The first sentence in the preceding paragraph is too often ignored.]

In dialogue, each speech, even if only a single word, is a paragraph by itself; that is, a new paragraph begins with each change of speaker. The application of this rule, when dialogue and narrative are combined, is best learned from examples in well-printed works of fiction.

[Once again, the goal is clarity and legibility.]

10. As a rule, begin each paragraph with a topic sentence; end it in conformity with the beginning.

Again, the object is to aid the reader. The practice here recommended enables him to discover the purpose of each paragraph as he begins to read it, and to retain the purpose in mind as he ends it. For this reason, the most generally useful kind of paragraph, particularly in exposition and argument, is that in which

1. the topic sentence comes at or near the beginning;

2. the succeeding sentences explain or establish or develop the statement made in the topic sentence; and

3. the final sentence either emphasizes the thought of the topic sentence or states some important consequence.

Ending with a digression, or with an unimportant detail, is particularly to be avoided.

If the paragraph forms part of a larger composition, its relation to what precedes, or its function as a part of the whole, may need to be expressed. This can sometimes be done by a mere word or phrase (*again*; *therefore*; *for the same reason*) in the topic sentence. Sometimes, however, it is expedient to precede the topic sentence by one or more sentences of introduction or transition. If more than one such sentence is required, it is generally better to set apart the transitional sentences as a separate paragraph.

According to the writer's purpose, he may, as indicated above, relate the body of the paragraph to the topic sentence in one or more of several different ways. He may make the meaning of the topic sentence clearer by restating it in other forms, by defining its terms, by denying the converse, by giving illustrations or specific instances; he may establish it by proofs; or he may develop it by showing its implications and consequences. In a long paragraph, he may carry out several of these processes.

[The annotator would prefer to see the next-to-last sentence split up into two or more sentences, and of course would prefer alternatives to *he* and *him*.]

1. Topic sentence.

Now, to be properly enjoyed,
a walking tour should be gone upon alone.

[*Now* as a transitional word to begin a sentence is always best followed by a comma.]

2. The meaning made clearer by denial of the contrary.

If you go in a company, or even in pairs,
it is no longer a walking tour in anything but name;
it is something else and more in the nature of a picnic.

3. The topic sentence repeated, in abridged form, and supported by three reasons; the meaning of the third ("you must have your own pace") made clearer by denying the converse.

A walking tour should be gone upon alone,
because freedom is of the essence; because you should be able
to stop and go on, and follow this way or that, as the freak takes you;
and because you must have your own pace,
and neither trot alongside a champion walker,
nor mince in time with a girl.

[*Freak*: whim. *Mince in time with a girl*: let us leave that one alone.]

4. A fourth reason, stated in two forms.

> And you must be open to all impressions
> and let your thoughts take colour from what you see.

[*Colour* is a holdover from British spelling. See "British spelling" in Usage.]

5. The same reason, stated in still another form.

> You should be as a pipe for any wind to play upon.

6.-7. The same reason as stated by Hazlitt.

> "I cannot see the wit," says Hazlitt,
> "of walking and talking at the same time."

[*Wit*: in archaic usage, a synonym for (good) sense, intelligence.]

> "When I am in the country, I wish to vegetate like the country,"
> which is the gist of all that can be said upon the matter.

[*Upon*: rather formal; *on* would do.]

8. Repetition, in paraphrase, of the quotation from Hazlitt.

> There should be no cackle of voices at your elbow,
> to jar on the meditative silence of the morning.

[Americans would now dispense with the comma after *elbow*.]

9. Final statement of the fourth reason, in language amplified and heightened to form a strong conclusion.

> "And so long as a man is reasoning he cannot surrender himself
> to that fine intoxication that comes of much motion in the open air, that
> begins in a sort of dazzle and sluggishness of the brain,
> and ends in a peace that passes comprehension."
> — Stevenson, *Walking Tours*.

1. Topic sentence.

It was chiefly in the eighteenth century
that a very different conception of history grew up.

[*Grew up*: nowadays, *arose*, *was developed*, or *came to the fore*.]

2. The meaning of the topic sentence made clearer; the new conception of history defined.

Historians then came to believe that their task was not so much
to paint a picture as to solve a problem; to explain or illustrate
the successive phases of national growth, prosperity, and adversity.

3. The definition expanded.

The history of morals, of industry, of intellect, and of art;
the changes that take place in manners or beliefs;
the dominant ideas that prevailed in successive periods;
the rise, fall, and modification of political constitutions;
in a word, all the conditions of national well-being
became the subjects of their works.

[Here, semicolons are appropriate, because the clauses have the sense of a list.]

4. The definition explained by contrast.

They sought rather to write a history of peoples
than a history of kings.

[The annotator would place *rather* after *peoples*.]

5. The definition supplemented: another element in the new conception of history.

They looked especially in history
for the chain of causes and effects.

[Previous page: Alternative: *they especially examined history.*]

6. Conclusion: an important consequence of the new conception of history.

"They undertook to study in the past the physiology of nations,
and hoped by applying the experimental method on a large scale
to deduce some lessons of real value about the conditions
on which the welfare of society mainly depend."
— Lecky, *The Political Value of History.*

In narration and description, the paragraph sometimes begins with a concise, comprehensive statement serving to hold together the details that follow.

The breeze served us admirably.
The campaign opened with a series of reverses.
The next ten or twelve pages were filled with a curious set of entries.

But this device, if too often used, would become a mannerism. More commonly the opening sentence simply indicates by its subject with what the paragraph is to be principally concerned.

At length I thought I might return towards the stockade.

[*Towards* is British usage, *toward*, American.]

He picked up the heavy lamp from the table
and began to explore.

[Whatever is done with *up* (in this case *heavy lamp up* seems acceptable), for drama I would insert a comma after *table*.]

Another flight of steps, and they emerged on the roof.

The brief paragraphs of animated narrative, however, are often without even this semblance of a topic sentence. The break between them serves the purpose of a rhetorical pause, throwing into prominence some detail of the action.

[Somehow, this could be clearer.]

11. Use the active voice.

The active voice is usually more direct and vigorous than the passive:

> I shall always remember my first visit to Boston.

This is much better than

> My first visit to Boston will always be remembered by me.

The latter sentence is less direct, less bold, and less concise. If the writer tries to make it more concise by omitting "by me,"

> My first visit to Boston will always be remembered,

it becomes indefinite: is it the writer, or some person undisclosed, or the world at large, that will always remember this visit?

This rule does not, of course, mean that the writer should entirely discard the passive voice, which is frequently convenient and sometimes necessary.

> The dramatists of the Restoration are little esteemed to-day.

[Today, *today*: an example of American English's penchant for dropping hyphens.]

> Modern readers have little esteem
> for the dramatists of the Restoration.

The first would be the right form in a paragraph on the dramatists of the Restoration; the second, in a paragraph on the tastes of modern readers. The need of making a particular word the subject of the sentence will often, as in these examples, determine which voice is to be used.

[For *need of making*, try *necessity of making*, or simply, *The word that is the subject*....]

The habitual use of the active voice, however, makes for forcible writing. This is true not only in narrative principally concerned with action, but in writing of any kind. Many a tame sentence of description or exposition can be made lively and emphatic by substituting a transitive in the active voice for some such perfunctory expression as *there is*, or *could be heard.*

[*Forcible*, here, means *effective, having force.*]

There were a great number of dead leaves lying on the ground.
Dead leaves covered the ground.

The sound of the falls could still be heard.
The sound of the falls still reached our ears.

The reason that he left college was that his health became impaired.
Failing health compelled him to leave college.

It was not long before he was very sorry that he had said what he had.
He soon repented his words.

As a rule, avoid making one passive depend directly upon another.

Gold was not allowed to be exported.
It was forbidden to export gold (The export of gold was prohibited).

He has been proved to have been seen entering the building.
It has been proved that he was seen to enter the building.

[In the correction to the last example, *seen entering* would currently be preferable.]

In both the examples above, before correction, the word properly related to the second passive is made the subject of the first.

A common fault is to use as the subject of a passive construction a noun which expresses the entire action, leaving to the verb no function beyond that of completing the sentence.

[In the following examples, the second versions are to be preferred.]

A survey of this region was made in 1900.
This region was surveyed in 1900.

Mobilization of the army was rapidly carried out.
The army was rapidly mobilized.

Confirmation of these reports cannot be obtained.
These reports cannot be confirmed.

Compare the sentence, "The export of gold was prohibited," in which the predicate *was prohibited* expresses something not implied in *export*.

[For *that* and *which*, see "that / which" in Usage.]

12. Put statements in positive form.

Make definite assertions. Avoid tame, colorless, hesitating, non-committal language. Use the word not as a means of denial or in antithesis, never as a means of evasion.

He was not very often on time.
He usually came late.

He did not think that studying Latin was much use.
He thought the study of Latin useless.

The Taming of the Shrew is rather weak in spots.
Shakespeare does not portray Katharine as a very admirable character, nor does Bianca remain long in memory as an important character in Shakespeare's works.

The women in *The Taming of the Shrew* are unattractive.
Katharine is disagreeable, Bianca insignificant.

The last example, before correction, is indefinite as well as negative. The corrected version, consequently, is simply a guess at the writer's intention.

[For notes on whether to use quotation marks or italics, see "quotation marks with other punctuation" in Usage.]

All three examples show the weakness inherent in the word *not*. Consciously or unconsciously, the reader is dissatisfied with being told only what is not; he wishes to be told what is. Hence, as a rule, it is better to express a negative in positive form.

not honest
dishonest

not important
trifling

did not remember
forgot

did not pay any attention to
ignored

did not have much confidence in
distrusted

The antithesis of negative and positive is strong:

Not charity, but simple justice.
Not that I loved Caesar less, but Rome the more.

Negative words other than *not* are usually strong:

The sun never sets upon the British flag.

13. Omit needless words.

Vigorous writing is concise. A sentence should contain no unnecessary words, a paragraph no unnecessary sentences, for the same reason that a drawing should have no unnecessary lines and a machine no unnecessary parts. This requires not that the writer make all his sentences short, or that he avoid all detail and treat his subjects only in outline, but that every word tell.

[The Plain Style again.]

Many expressions in common use violate this principle:

[Again, the second versions are preferable to the first.]

the question as to whether
whether (the question whether)

there is no doubt but that
no doubt (doubtless)

used for fuel purposes
used for fuel

he is a man who
he

in a hasty manner
hastily

this is a subject which
this subject

His story is a strange one.
His story is strange.

In especial the expression *the fact that* should be revised out of every sentence in which it occurs.

[The sentence, which is already emphatic, doesn't need the archaic-sounding first two words.]

owing to the fact that
since (because)

in spite of the fact that
though (although)

call your attention to the fact that
remind you (notify you)

I was unaware of the fact that
I was unaware that (did not know)

the fact that he had not succeeded
his failure

the fact that I had arrived
my arrival

See also under *case, character, nature, system* in Chapter V.

Who is, which was, and the like are often superfluous.

His brother, who is a member of the same firm
His brother, a member of the same firm

Trafalgar, which was Nelson's last battle
Trafalgar, Nelson's last battle

As positive statement is more concise than negative, and the active voice more concise than the passive, many of the examples given under Rules 11 and 12 illustrate this rule as well.

A common violation of conciseness is the presentation of a single complex idea, step by step, in a series of sentences which might to advantage be combined into one.

Macbeth was very ambitious. This led him to wish to become
king of Scotland. The witches told him that this wish of his
would come true. The king of Scotland at this time
was Duncan. Encouraged by his wife, Macbeth murdered Duncan.
He was thus enabled to succeed Duncan as king. (*55 words.*)

Encouraged by his wife, Macbeth achieved his ambition
and realized the prediction of the witches by murdering Duncan
and becoming king of Scotland in his place. (*26 words.*)

14. Avoid a succession of loose sentences.

This rule refers especially to loose sentences of a particular type, those consisting of two co-ordinate clauses, the second introduced by a conjunction or relative. Although single sentences of this type may be unexceptionable (see under Rule 4), a series soon becomes monotonous and tedious.

An unskilful writer will sometimes construct a whole paragraph of sentences of this kind, using as connectives *and*, *but*, and less frequently, *who*, *which*, *when*, *where*, and *while*, these last in non-restrictive senses (see under Rule 3).

> The third concert of the subscription series was given last evening, and a large audience was in attendance. Mr. Edward Appleton was the soloist, and the Boston Symphony Orchestra furnished the instrumental music. The former showed himself to be an artist of the first rank, while the latter proved itself fully deserving of its high reputation. The interest aroused by the series has been very gratifying to the Committee, and it is planned to give a similar series annually hereafter. The fourth concert will be given on Tuesday, May 10, when an equally attractive programme will be presented.

Apart from its triteness and emptiness, the paragraph above is bad because of the structure of its sentences, with their mechanical symmetry and singsong. Contrast with them the sentences in the paragraphs quoted under Rule 10, or in any piece of good English prose, as the preface (*Before the Curtain*) to *Vanity Fair*.

If the writer finds that he has written a series of sentences of the type described, he should recast enough of them to remove the monotony, replacing them by simple sentences, by sentences of two clauses joined by a semicolon, by periodic sentences of two clauses, by sentences, loose or periodic, of three clauses—whichever best represent the real relations of the thought.

[*Unskilful, passim*: The annotator prefers to see the root word in the adjective; thus, *skillful*, and *willful*.]

15. Express co-ordinate ideas in similar form.

[Nowadays, *coordinate*: equal in rank or importance.]

This principle, that of parallel construction, requires that expressions of similar content and function should be outwardly similar. The likeness of form enables the reader to recognize more readily the likeness of content and function. Familiar instances from the Bible are the Ten Commandments, the Beatitudes, and the petitions of the Lord's Prayer.

The unskilful writer often violates this principle, from a mistaken belief that he should constantly vary the form of his expressions. It is true that in repeating a statement in order to emphasize it he may have need to vary its form. For illustration, see the paragraph from Stevenson quoted under Rule 10. But apart from this, he should follow the principle of parallel construction.

> Formerly, science was taught by the textbook method,
> while now the laboratory method is employed.

> Formerly, science was taught by the textbook method;
> now it is taught by the laboratory method.

The left-hand [here, first] version gives the impression that the writer is undecided or timid; he seems unable or afraid to choose one form of expression and hold to it. The right-hand [here, second] version shows that the writer has at least made his choice and abided by it.

By this principle, an article or a preposition applying to all the members of a series must either be used only before the first term or else be repeated before each term.

> The French, the Italians, Spanish, and Portuguese
> The French, the Italians, the Spanish, and the Portuguese

> In spring, summer, or in winter
> In spring, summer, or winter (In spring, in summer, or in winter)

Correlative expressions (*both, and*; *not, but*; *not only, but also*; *either, or*; *first, second, third*; and the like) should be followed by the same grammatical construction. Many violations of this rule can be corrected by rearranging the sentence.

It was both a long ceremony and very tedious.
The ceremony was both long and tedious.

A time not for words, but action
A time not for words, but for action

Either you must grant his request or incur his ill will.
You must either grant his request or incur his ill will.

My objections are, first, the injustice of the measure;
second, that it is unconstitutional.

My objections are, first, that the measure is unjust;
second, that it is unconstitutional.

See also the third example under Rule 12 and the last under Rule 13.

It may be asked, what if a writer needs to express a very large number of similar ideas, say twenty? Must he write twenty consecutive sentences of the same pattern? On closer examination he will probably find that the difficulty is imaginary, that his twenty ideas can be classified in groups, and that he need apply the principle only within each group. Otherwise he had best avoid the difficulty by putting his statements in the form of a table.

16. Keep related words together.

The position of the words in a sentence is the principal means of showing their relationship. The writer must therefore, so far as possible, bring together the words, and groups of words, that are related in thought, and keep apart those which are not so related.

[*So far as possible* is often stronger than *as far as possible*. See "so far as / as far as" in Usage.]

The subject of a sentence and the principal verb should not, as a rule, be separated by a phrase or clause that can be transferred to the beginning.

Wordsworth, in the fifth book of *The Excursion,*
gives a minute description of this church.

In the fifth book of *The Excursion,*
Wordsworth gives a minute description of this church.

Cast iron, when treated in a Bessemer converter,
is changed into steel.

By treatment in a Bessemer converter,
cast iron is changed into steel.

The objection is that the interposed phrase or clause needlessly interrupts the natural order of the main clause. This objection, however, does not usually hold when the order is interrupted only by a relative clause or by an expression in apposition. Nor does it hold in periodic sentences in which the interruption is a deliberately used means of creating suspense (see examples under Rule 18).

[For the definition of *apposition*, see page 11.]

The relative pronoun should come, as a rule, immediately after its antecedent.

There was a look in his eye that boded mischief.
In his eye was a look that boded mischief.

He wrote three articles about his adventures in Spain,
which were published in *Harper's Magazine.*

He published in *Harper's Magazine* three articles
about his adventures in Spain.

[In these examples, the annotator prefers the first versions.]

This is a portrait of Benjamin Harrison, grandson of
William Henry Harrison, who became President in 1889.

This is a portrait of Benjamin Harrison, grandson of
William Henry Harrison. He became President in 1889.

If the antecedent consists of a group of words, the relative comes at the end of the group, unless this would cause ambiguity.

[*Relative*, here, means a clause introduced by the relative pronouns, *who* or *which*.]

The Superintendent of the Chicago Division, who

A proposal to amend the Sherman Act,
which has been variously judged

A proposal, which has been variously judged,
to amend the Sherman Act

A proposal to amend the Sherman Act, which has been variously judged
[*an improvement, with changed wording:*]
A proposal to amend the much-debated Sherman Act

The grandson of William Henry Harrison, who
William Henry Harrison's grandson, Benjamin Harrison, who

A noun in apposition may come between antecedent and relative, because in such a combination no real ambiguity can arise.

The Duke of York, his brother,
who was regarded with hostility by the Whigs

[*Apposition*: page 11.]

Modifiers should come, if possible, next to the word they modify. If several expressions modify the same word, they should be so arranged that no wrong relation is suggested.

All the members were not present.
Not all the members were present.

He only found two mistakes.
He found only two mistakes.

[The correct placement of *only* is so often ignored that it deserves a separate jeremiad. See "only" in Usage, and "If Only...." in the Rogue's Gallery.]

> Major R. E. Joyce will give a lecture on Tuesday evening
> in Bailey Hall, to which the public is invited,
> on "My Experiences in Mesopotamia" at eight P.M.

> On Tuesday evening at eight P. M.,
> Major R. E. Joyce will give in Bailey Hall a lecture on
> "My Experiences in Mesopotamia." The public is invited.

17. In summaries, keep to one tense.

In summarizing the action of a drama, the writer should always use the present tense. In summarizing a poem, story, or novel, he should preferably use the present, though he may use the past if he prefers. If the summary is in the present tense, antecedent action should be expressed by the perfect; if in the past, by the past perfect.

[*The perfect*, i.e., *the present perfect*: **If the writing is in the present tense but something is referred to that took place in the past, the defining verb is coupled with *has* or *have*. "I *have* seen that movie many times." *Past perfect*: If the writing is in the past tense, the thing that took place earlier is coupled with *had*. "He explained that he *had* seen that movie many times."**]

> An unforeseen chance prevents Friar John from delivering
> Friar Lawrence's letter to Romeo. Juliet, meanwhile, owing to
> her father's arbitrary change of the day set for her wedding,
> has been compelled to drink the potion on Tuesday night,
> with the result that Balthasar informs Romeo of her supposed death
> before Friar Lawrence learns of the non-delivery of the letter.

[*Chance*: **Something that happens unpredictably, without discernible human intention or observable cause. Rare. Nowadays we would probably say *circumstance* or *accident*, or change the sentence to read: "Something unforeseen keeps Friar John from...."**]

But whichever tense be used in the summary, a past tense in indirect discourse or in indirect question remains unchanged.

[*Be used*: **A rigorous use of the subjunctive (which see in Usage).**]

The Legate inquires who struck the blow.

[*Legate*: **An emissary, usually official.**]

Apart from the exceptions noted, whichever tense the writer chooses, he should use throughout. Shifting from one tense to the other gives the appearance of uncertainty and irresolution (compare Rule 15).

In presenting the statements or the thought of some one else, as in summarizing an essay or reporting a speech, the writer should avoid intercalating such expressions as *he said, he stated, the speaker added, the speaker then went on to say, the author also thinks*, or the like. He should indicate clearly at the outset, once for all, that what follows is summary, and then waste no words in repeating the notification.

[*Some one*: **Once correct; now, of course,** *someone*. **For other words that have been similarly compressed, see "any more / anymore" in Usage.** *Intercalate*: **insert.**]

In notebooks, in newspapers, in handbooks of literature, summaries of one kind or another may be indispensable, and for children in primary schools it is a useful exercise to retell a story in their own words. But in the criticism or interpretation of literature the writer should be careful to avoid dropping into summary. He may find it necessary to devote one or two sentences to indicating the subject, or the opening situation, of the work he is discussing; he may cite numerous details to illustrate its qualities. But he should aim to write an orderly discussion supported by evidence, not a summary with occasional comment. Similarly, if the scope of his discussion includes a number of works, he will as a rule do better not to take them up singly in chronological order, but to aim from the beginning at establishing general conclusions.

18. Place the emphatic words of a sentence at the end.

The proper place for the word, or group of words, which the writer desires to make most prominent is usually the end of the sentence.

> Humanity has hardly advanced in fortitude since that time,
> though it has advanced in many other ways.

> Humanity, since that time, has advanced in many other ways,
> but it has hardly advanced in fortitude.

> This steel is principally used for making razors,
> because of its hardness.

> Because of its hardness,
> this steel is principally used in making razors.

[For *though* and *although*, see "although / though" in Usage.]

The word or group of words entitled to this position of prominence is usually the logical predicate, that is, the new element in the sentence, as it is in the second example.

[*Predicate*: The part of a sentence or clause that expresses what is said of the subject; usually it contains a verb.]

The effectiveness of the periodic sentence arises from the prominence which it gives to the main statement.

[*Periodic sentence*: A sentence that is not grammatically complete until the very end, i.e., until it reaches its *period*. By holding an idea in suspense, it arouses interest and curiosity. Following are two examples.]

> Four centuries ago, Christopher Columbus,
> one of the Italian mariners whom the decline of their own republics
> had put at the service of the world and of adventure,
> seeking for Spain a westward passage to the Indies as a set-off
> against the achievements of Portuguese discoverers, lighted on America.

> With these hopes and in this belief I would urge you,
> laying aside all hindrance, thrusting away all private aims,
> to devote yourselves unswervingly and unflinchingly
> to the vigorous and successful prosecution of this war.

The other prominent position in the sentence is the beginning. Any element in the sentence, other than the subject, becomes emphatic when placed first.

> Deceit or treachery he could never forgive.

> So vast and rude, fretted by the action of nearly three thousand years,
> the fragments of this architecture may often seem,
> at first sight, like works of nature.

A subject coming first in its sentence may be emphatic, but hardly by its position alone. In the sentence,

> Great kings worshipped at his shrine,

the emphasis upon kings arises largely from its meaning and from the context. To receive special emphasis, the subject of a sentence must take the position of the predicate.

> Through the middle of the valley flowed a winding stream.

[*Context*, above: wildly and irresponsibly overused (though not here). See "context" in Usage.]

The principle that the proper place for what is to be made most prominent is the end applies equally to the words of a sentence, to the sentences of a paragraph, and to the paragraphs of a composition.

IV. A Few Matters of Form

Headings. Leave a blank line, or its equivalent in space, after the title or heading of a manuscript. On succeeding pages, if using ruled paper, begin on the first line.

Numerals. Do not spell out dates or other serial numbers. Write them in figures or in Roman notation, as may be appropriate.

August 9, 1918
Chapter XII
Rule 3
352d Infantry

[Nowadays, *352nd* Infantry, as in 2nd Infantry Division. No one would kill you for writing *Chapter Twelve*, and *Rule Three*. The British would tend to write *9 August 1918*.]

Parentheses. A sentence containing an expression in parenthesis is punctuated, outside of the marks of parenthesis, exactly as if the expression in parenthesis were absent. The expression within is punctuated as if it stood by itself, except that the final stop is omitted unless it is a question mark or an exclamation point.

I went to his house yesterday (my third attempt to see him),
but he had left town.

He declares (and why should we doubt his good faith?)
that he is now certain of success.

(When a wholly detached expression or sentence is parenthesized, the final stop comes before the last mark of parenthesis.)

[As here: the stop—the period—is inside the parenthesis.]

Quotations. Formal quotations, cited as documentary evidence, are introduced by a colon and enclosed in quotation marks.

The provision of the Constitution is:
"No tax or duty shall be laid on articles exported from any state."

Quotations grammatically in apposition or the direct objects of verbs are preceded by a comma and enclosed in quotation marks.

I recall the maxim of La Rochefoucauld,
"Gratitude is a lively sense of benefits to come."

Aristotle says, "Art is an imitation of nature."

[*Grammatically in apposition*: each sentence has two elements, the second of which defines, explains, or illustrates—is the reason for—the first; they have equal importance, and equal weight.]

Quotations of an entire line, or more, of verse, are begun on a fresh line and centered, but need not be enclosed in quotation marks.

Wordsworth's enthusiasm for the Revolution was at first unbounded:

Bliss was it in that dawn to be alive,
But to be young was very heaven!

[A single line can also be placed within the text, between quotation marks. Two or more lines within the text can be separated by a / (virgule, or slash); the annotator prefers a space before and after it.]

Quotations introduced by *that* are regarded as in indirect discourse and not enclosed in quotation marks.

Keats declares that beauty is truth, truth beauty.

Proverbial expressions and familiar phrases of literary origin require no quotation marks.

These are the times that try men's souls.

He lives far from the madding crowd.

The same is true of colloquialisms and slang.

References. In scholarly work requiring exact references, abbreviate titles that occur frequently, giving the full forms in an alphabetical list at the end. As a general practice, give the references in parenthesis or in footnotes, not in the body of the sentence. Omit the words *act, scene, line, book, volume, page,* except when referring [to the text] by only one of them. Punctuate as indicated below.

[The thought (which can also be set off by commas or dashes) is the *parenthesis*; the curly brackets are the *parentheses*.]

In the second scene of the third act

In *III.ii* (still better, simply insert *III.ii* in parentheses at the proper place in the sentence).

After the killing of Polonius,
Hamlet is placed under guard (IV. ii. 14).

2 Samuel i:17-27

Othello II.iii 264-267, III.iii. 155-161

[Nowadays, 2 Samuel, I:17-27. The choice of the best form will probably depend on the number of citations.]

Titles. For the titles of literary works, scholarly usage prefers italics with capitalized initials. The usage of editors and publishers varies, some using italics with capitalized initials, others using Roman with capitalized initials and with or without quotation marks. Use italics (indicated in manuscript by underscoring), except in writing for a periodical that follows a different practice. Omit initial *A* or *The* from titles when you place the possessive before them.

The Iliad; the Odyssey; As You Like It; To a Skylark; The Newcomes; A Tale of Two Cities; Dickens's *Tale of Two Cities.*

[Nowadays, *The Odyssey*, and "To a Skylark." In general, short stories and short poems take quotation marks, longer poems, *italics*; plays take *italics*. For more, see "quotation marks with other punctuation" in Usage. *Roman*: normal text, not *italics*.]

V. Words and Expressions Commonly Misused

(Many of the words and expressions here listed are not so much bad English as bad style, the commonplaces of careless writing. As illustrated under *Feature*, the proper correction is likely to be not the replacement of one word or set of words by another, but the replacement of vague generality by definite statement.)

[The annotator suggests that an entire paragraph, especially one beginning a chapter or section, should never be enclosed in parentheses.]

All right. Idiomatic in familiar speech as a detached phrase in the sense, *Agreed*, or *Go ahead*. In other uses better avoided. Always written as two words.

[Always. Never *alright*.]

As good or better than. Expressions of this type should be corrected by rearranging the sentence.

My opinion is as good or better than his.
My opinion is as good as his, or better (if not better).

As to whether. *Whether* is sufficient; see under Rule 13.

Bid. Takes the infinitive without *to*. The past tense is *bade*.

[This entry grates the cheese rather thinly. The past tense can also be *bid*: "He bid two hearts." *Bid* also takes *for*: "He bid for the contract." "She bid for a place on the varsity."]

But. Unnecessary after *doubt* and *help*.

I have no doubt but that
I have no doubt that

He could not help see but that
He could not help seeing that

The too frequent use of *but* as a conjunction leads to the fault discussed under Rule 14. A loose sentence formed with *but* can always be converted into a periodic sentence formed with *although*, as illustrated under Rule 4.

Particularly awkward is the following of one *but* by another, making a contrast to a contrast or a reservation to a reservation. This is easily corrected by rearrangement.

America had vast resources, but she seemed almost wholly
unprepared for war. But within a year she had created
an army of four million men.

America seemed almost wholly unprepared for war,
but she had vast resources. Within a year she had created
an army of four million men.

[See "can't help but" in Usage.]

Can. Means *am* (*is*, *are*) able. Not to be used as a substitute for *may*.

[The classic example is: "Can I drive your car?" "Yes you *can*." (I'm aware that you know how to drive.) "*May* you drive my car? No, you *may* not." In the real world, the usages often overlap.]

Case. *The Concise Oxford Dictionary* begins its definition of this word: *instance of a thing's occurring*; *usual state of affairs*. In these two senses, the word is usually unnecessary.

In many cases, the rooms were poorly ventilated.
Many of the rooms were poorly ventilated.

It has rarely been the case that any mistake has been made.
Few mistakes have been made.

See Wood, *Suggestions to Authors*, pp. 68-71, and Quiller-Couch, *The Art of Writing*, pp. 103-106.

Certainly. Used indiscriminately by some writers, much as others use *very*, to intensify any and every statement. A mannerism of this kind, bad in speech, is even worse in writing.

Character. Often simply redundant, used from a mere habit of wordiness.

Acts of a hostile character
Hostile acts

Claim, vb. With object-noun, means *lay claim to*. May be used with a dependent clause if this sense is clearly involved: "He claimed that he was the sole surviving heir." (But even here, *claimed to be* would be better.) Not to be used as a substitute for *declare*, *maintain*, or *charge*.

[*Vb.*: Verb. It would be improper to say, e.g., "He claims that there are *six* Great Lakes." On the other hand, when an element of doubt is involved, *claim* can substitute for *maintain*. "He claims that at the time the robbery was committed, he was at a friend's house."]

Clever. This word has been greatly overused; it is best restricted to *ingenuity displayed in small matters*.

[i.e., avoid *clever* as a catch-all word when *imaginative, inventive, ingenious*, or some such, would be more accurate.]

Compare. To *compare to* is to point out or imply resemblances, between objects regarded as essentially of different order; to *compare with* is mainly to point out differences, between objects regarded as essentially of the same order. Thus life has been *compared to* a pilgrimage, to a drama, to a battle; Congress may be *compared with* the British Parliament. Paris has been *compared to* ancient Athens; it may be *compared with* modern London.

[Similarly with *relation to*, *relation with*. See "compare to / compare with" in Usage.]

Consider. Not followed by *as* when it means, *believe to be.* "I consider him thoroughly competent." Compare, "The lecturer considered Cromwell first as soldier and second as administrator," where *considered* means *examined* or *discussed.*

Data. A plural, like *phenomena* and *strata.*

[e.g., "The data on the subject *are* ambiguous." Also acceptable: "The data [here, a *mass noun*] *is* inconclusive."]

Dependable. A needless substitute for *reliable, trustworthy.*

Different than. Not permissible. Substitute *different from, other than,* or *unlike.*

[A distinction worth making, but the rule is needlessly strict. In many instances, *than* is perfectly acceptable, even necessary. "I am no different *than* you." "Things are different *than* they used to be."]

Divided into. Not to be misused for *composed of.* The line is sometimes difficult to draw; doubtless plays are *divided into* acts, but poems are *composed of* stanzas.

Due to. Incorrectly used for *through, because of,* or *owing to,* in adverbial phrases: "He lost the first game, *due to* carelessness." In correct use related as predicate or as modifier to a particular noun: "This invention is *due to* Edison"; "losses *due to* preventable fires."

[For more, see "due to / owing to" in Usage.]

Effect. As noun, means *result*; as verb, means *to bring about, accomplish* (not to be confused with *affect,* which means *to influence*).

As noun, often loosely used in perfunctory writing about fashions, music, painting, and other arts: *an Oriental effect; effects in pale green; very delicate effects; broad effects; subtle effects; a charming effect was produced by.* The writer who has a definite meaning to express will not take refuge in such vagueness.

[For more, see "affect / effect" in Usage.]

Etc. Not to be used of persons. Equivalent to *and the rest, and so forth,* and hence not to be used if one of these would be insufficient, that is, if the reader would be left in doubt as to any important particulars. Least open to objection when it represents the last terms of a list already given in full, or immaterial words at the end of a quotation.

At the end of a list introduced by *such as, for example,* or any similar expression, *etc.* is incorrect.

[*Etc.* passes muster in casual writing, e.g., letters, never in formal. See "etc." in Usage.]

Fact. Use this word only of matters of a kind capable of direct verification, not of matters of judgment. That a particular event happened on a given date, that lead melts at a certain temperature, are facts. But such conclusions as that Napoleon was the greatest of modern generals, or that the climate of California is delightful, however incontestable they may be, are not properly facts.

On the formula *the fact that,* see under Rule 13.

Factor. A hackneyed word; the expressions of which it forms part can usually be replaced by something more direct and idiomatic.

> His superior training was the great factor
> in his winning the match.

> He won the match by being better trained.

> Heavy artillery is becoming an increasingly important factor
> in deciding battles.

> Heavy artillery is playing a larger and larger part
> in deciding battles.

[A further thought at "factors" in Usage.]

Feature. Another hackneyed word; like *factor* it usually adds nothing to the sentence in which it occurs.

> A feature of the entertainment especially
> worthy of mention was the singing of Miss A.

(Better use the same number of words to tell what Miss A. sang, or if the programme has already been given, to tell something of *how* she sang.)

As a verb, in the advertising sense of *offer as a special attraction*, to be avoided.

[It is now acceptable to write, as well as say, "The living room features brand new track lighting." *Programme*: British spelling.]

Fix. Colloquial in America for *arrange, prepare, mend*. In writing restrict it to its literary senses, *fasten, make firm or immovable*, etc.

[In all its many senses, *fix* is a perfectly good word. Precisely because it *has* so many meanings, however, a careful writer will first look for a more exact, more expressive synonym.]

Get. The colloquial *have got* for *have* should not be used in writing. The preferable form of the participle is *got*.

[In most instances, the annotator prefers *gotten* to *got*. The British would say, "He has *got* in with the wrong crowd," most Americans, "he has *gotten* in...."]

He is a man who. A common type of redundant expression; see Rule 13.

> He is a man who is very ambitious.
> He is very ambitious.

> Spain is a country which I have always wanted to visit.
> I have always wanted to visit Spain.

However. In the meaning *nevertheless*, not to come first in its sentence or clause.

> The roads were almost impassable.
> However, we at last succeeded in reaching camp.

> The roads were almost impassable.
> At last, however, we succeeded in reaching camp.

When *however* comes first, it means *in whatever way* or *to whatever extent.*

> However you advise him, he will probably do as he thinks best.
> However discouraging the prospect, he never lost heart.

[Some leeway, here, is now permissible.]

Interesting. Avoid this word as a perfunctory means of introduction. Instead of announcing that what you are about to tell is interesting, make it so.

> An interesting story is told of

(Tell the story without preamble.)

> In connection with the anticipated visit of Mr. B. to America,
> it is interesting to recall that he

> Mr. B., who it is expected will soon visit America

Kind of. Not to be used as a substitute for *rather* (before adjectives and verbs), or except in familiar style, *for something like* (before nouns). Restrict it to its literal sense: "Amber is a kind of fossil resin"; "I dislike that kind of notoriety." The same holds true of *sort of.*

["She's *kind of* (*sort of*) pretty," and "that *kind of* (*sort of*) birdhouse," for example, aren't appropriate in formal writing.]

Less. Should not be misused for *fewer*.

> He had less men than in the previous campaign.
> He had fewer men than in the previous campaign.

Less refers to quantity, *fewer* to number. "His troubles are less than mine" means "His troubles are not so great as mine." "His troubles are fewer than mine" means "His troubles are not so numerous as mine." It is, however, correct to say, "The signers of the petition were less than a hundred," where the round number, *a hundred*, is something like a collective noun, and *less* is thought of as meaning *a less quantity or amount*.

[To the irritation of sticklers, express lines at supermarket checkouts now typically say "Eight Items or Less," and we ask friends to express thoughts "in twenty-five words or less." The matter is amplified, and *collective noun* explained, at "less / fewer" in the Supplement to Usage.]

Like. Not to be misused for *as*. *Like* governs nouns and pronouns; before phrases and clauses the equivalent word is *as*.

> We spent the evening like in the old days.
> We spent the evening as in the old days.

> He thought like I did.
> He thought as I did (like me).

[In other words, something is *like* something else, but one *does* something exactly *as* one did it last year. See "like / as" in Usage.]

Line, along these lines. *Line* in the sense of course of *procedure, conduct, thought*, is allowable, but has been so much overworked, particularly in the phrase *along these lines*, that a writer who aims at freshness or originality had better discard it entirely.

> Mr. B. also spoke along the same lines.
> Mr. B. also spoke, to the same effect.

> He is studying along the line of French literature.
> He is studying French literature.

Literal, literally. Often incorrectly used in support of exaggeration or violent metaphor.

A literal flood of abuse
A flood of abuse

Literally dead with fatigue
Almost dead with fatigue (dead tired)

[A common (and thoughtless) error. Cf. "literally" in Usage.]

Lose out. Meant to be more emphatic than *lose*, but actually less so, because of its commonness. The same holds true of *try out, win out, sign up, register up.* With a number of verbs, *out* and *up* form idiomatic combinations: *find out, run out, turn out, cheer up, dry up, make up,* and others, each distinguishable in meaning from the simple verb. *Lose out* is not.

[There are many similar, and often needless, redundancies: *shrink down, reinstall again, collaborate together, revert back, same exact....*]

Most. Not to be used for *almost.*

Most everybody
Almost everybody

Most all the time
Almost all the time

[This injunction applies less to spoken English than to written.]

Nature. Often simply redundant, used like *character.*

Acts of a hostile nature
Hostile acts

Often vaguely used in such expressions as *a lover of nature*; *poems about nature.* Unless more specific statements follow, the reader cannot tell whether the poems have to do with natural scenery, rural life, the sunset, the untracked wilderness, or the habits of squirrels.

["Nature" lovers, and writers about "nature," take note.]

Near by. Adverbial phrase, not yet fully accepted as good English, though the analogy of *close by* and *hard by* seems to justify it. *Near*, or *near at hand*, is as good, if not better.

Not to be used as an adjective; use *neighboring*.

[*Nearby*, one word, is now acceptable in sentences like "Nearby, there was a beautiful lake."]

Oftentimes, ofttimes. Archaic forms, no longer in good use. The modern word is *often*.

[*Often*: The word is most properly pronounced to rhyme with *soften*.]

One hundred and one. Retain the *and* in this and similar expressions, in accordance with the unvarying usage of English prose from Old English times.

[e.g., "One hundred and twenty-five," "two hundred and twelve...."]

One of the most. Avoid beginning essays or paragraphs with this formula, as, "One of the most interesting developments of modern science is, etc."; "Switzerland is one of the most interesting countries of Europe." There is nothing wrong in this; it is simply threadbare and forcible-feeble.

A common blunder is to use a singular verb in a relative clause following *this* or a similar expression, when the relative is the subject.

One of the ablest men that *has* attacked this problem.
One of the ablest men that *have* attacked this problem.

[Previous page: *Forcible-feeble*: Strunk's idiosyncrasy. Nowadays we would say, simply, *feeble*, and save *forcible* for phrases like, "a *forcible* entry into the house."]

Participle for verbal noun.

Do you mind me asking a question?
Do you mind my asking a question?

There was little prospect of the Senate
accepting even this compromise.

There was little prospect of the Senate's
accepting even this compromise.

In the first version of each example, *asking* and *accepting* are present participles; in the second versions, they are verbal nouns (*gerunds*). The construction shown in the first version is occasionally found, and has its defenders. Yet it is easy to see that the second sentence has to do not with a prospect of the Senate, but with a prospect of accepting. In this example, at least, the [first] construction is plainly illogical.

As the authors of *The King's English* point out, there are sentences apparently, but not really, of this type, in which the possessive is not called for.

I cannot imagine Lincoln refusing
his assent to this measure.

In this sentence, what the writer cannot imagine is Lincoln himself, in the act of refusing his assent. Yet the meaning would be virtually the same, except for a slight loss of vividness, if he had written,

I cannot imagine Lincoln's refusing
his assent to this measure.

By using the possessive, the writer will always be on the safe side. In the examples above, the subject of the action is a single, unmodified term, immediately preceding the verbal noun, and the construction is as good as any that could be used. But in any sentence in which it is a mere clumsy substitute for something simpler, or in which the use of the possessive is awkward or impossible, should of course be recast.

In the event of a reconsideration of the whole matter's
becoming necessary

If it should become necessary to reconsider
the whole matter

There was great dissatisfaction with the decision
of the arbitrators being favorable to the company.

There was great dissatisfaction that the arbitrators
should have decided in favor of the company.

[See "possessives modifying gerunds," in Usage. *The King's English*: a
book by H. W. and F. G. Fowler, published in 1906. The former (*q.v.*)
became a notable authority on grammar, style, and usage.]

People. *The people* is a political term, not to be confused with *the public.*
From *the people* comes political support or opposition; from *the public*
comes artistic appreciation or commercial patronage.

The word *people* is not to be used with words of number, in place of
persons. If of "six people" five went away, how many "people" would be
left?

[More at "persons / people" in Usage.]

Phase. Means *a stage of transition or development: the phases of the
moon; the last phase.* Not to be used for *aspect* or *topic.*

Another phase of the subject
Another point (another question)

Possess. Not to be used as a mere substitute for *have* or *own.*

He possessed great courage.
He had great courage (was very brave).

He was the fortunate possessor of
He owned

Prove. The past participle is *proved*.

[*Proven* is now also acceptable. See "proved / proven" in Usage.]

Respective, respectively. These words may usually be omitted with advantage.

> Works of fiction are listed under the names of their respective authors.
> Works of fiction are listed under the names of their authors.

> The one mile and two mile runs were won
> by Jones and Cummings respectively.

> The one mile and two mile runs were won
> by Jones and by Cummings.

In some kinds of formal writing, as in geometrical proofs, it may be necessary to use *respectively*, but it should not appear in writing on ordinary subjects.

[*One mile...two mile*: These are not adjectival, not descriptions, but names of events, therefore not hyphenated. Cf. *the hundred yard dash.*]

Shall, Will. The future tense requires *shall* for the first person, *will* for the second and third. The formula to express the speaker's belief regarding his future action or state is *I shall*; *I will* expresses his determination or his consent.

[*I shall*, common in England, retains a bit of spunk and panache that *I will* doesn't have, but in America it is now generally replaced by *I will*: "*I will* bring some food." *I shall*, however, still has its uses: "I *shall* return" (General Douglas MacArthur). "I *shall* be pleased to do that for you." Cf. "She was, *shall* we say...." "*Shall* we go?" Note that the peace movement anthem is "We *Shall* Overcome."]

Should. See under *Would*.

So. Avoid, in writing, the use of *so* as an intensifier: *so good*; *so warm*; *so delightful.*

On the use of *so* to introduce clauses, see Rule 4.

Sort of. See under *Kind of.*

Split Infinitive. There is precedent from the fourteenth century downward for interposing an adverb between *to* and the infinitive which it governs, but the construction is in disfavor and is avoided by nearly all careful writers.

> To diligently inquire
> To inquire diligently

[Another preferred form is *diligently to inquire*: "He resolved *diligently to inquire* into the circumstances that made the accident possible." See "Split infinitives" in Usage, and "Split Ends and Split Infinitives" in the Rouge's Gallery.]

State. Not to be used as a mere substitute for *say, remark*. Restrict it to the sense of *express fully or clearly*, as, "He refused to state his objections."

Student body. A needless and awkward expression, meaning no more than the simple word *students*.

> A member of the student body
> A student
>
> Popular with the student body
> Liked by the students
>
> The student body passed resolutions.
> The students passed resolutions.

[For *student body*, Strunk favored *studentry*.]

System. Frequently used without need.

Dayton has adopted the commission system of government.
Dayton has adopted government by commission.

The dormitory system
Dormitories

[*Without need*: i.e., when redundant and unnecessary. While we're on the subject of education, the phrase *physical plant*, to refer to the buildings and grounds of a campus, always seemed to the annotator grotesque.]

Thanking you in advance. This sounds as if the writer meant, *It will not be worth my while to write to you again.* Simply write, *Thanking you*, and if the favor which you have requested is granted, write a letter of acknowledgment.

[Or simply, *thank you*.]

They. A common inaccuracy is the use of the plural pronoun when the antecedent is a distributive expression such as *each, each one, everybody, every one, many a man*, which, though implying more than one person, requires the pronoun to be in the singular. Similar to this, but with even less justification, is the use of the plural pronoun with the antecedent *anybody, any one, somebody, some one*, the intention being either to avoid the awkward *he or she*, or to avoid committing oneself to either. Some bashful speakers even say, *A friend of mine told me that they, etc.*

Use *he* with all the above words, unless the antecedent is or must be feminine.

[Times have changed. See discussion at "his, hers / their" in Usage.]

Very. Use this word sparingly. Where emphasis is necessary, use words strong in themselves.

Viewpoint. Write *point of view,* but do not misuse this, as many do, for *view* or *opinion.*

[This now seems rather stringent. Cf. "stance" in Usage.]

While. Avoid the indiscriminate use of this word for *and, but,* and *although.* Many writers use it frequently as a substitute for *and* or *but,* either from a mere desire to vary the connective, or from uncertainty which of the two connectives is the more appropriate. In this use it is best replaced by a semicolon.

> The office and salesrooms are on the ground floor,
> while the rest of the building is devoted to manufacturing.

> The office and salesrooms are on the ground floor;
> the rest of the building is devoted to manufacturing.

Its use as a virtual equivalent of *although* is allowable in sentences where this leads to no ambiguity or absurdity.

> While I admire his energy,
> I wish it were employed in a better cause.

This is entirely correct, as shown by the paraphrase,

> I admire his energy; at the same time
> I wish it were employed in a better cause.

Compare:

> While the temperature reaches 90 or 95 degrees in the daytime
> the nights are often chilly.

> Although the temperature reaches 90 or 95 degrees in the daytime,
> the nights are often chilly.

The paraphrase,

> The temperature reaches 90 or 95 degrees in the daytime;
> at the same time the nights are often chilly,

shows why the use of *while* is incorrect. In general, the writer will do well to use *while* only with strict literalness, in the sense of *during the time that.*

[Nowadays, "While I agree with your point..." seems acceptable. See "although / though" in Usage.]

Whom. Often incorrectly used for *who* before *he said* or similar expressions, when it is really the subject of a following verb.

> His brother, whom he said would send him the money
> His brother, who he said would send him the money

> The man whom he thought was his friend
> The man who (that) he thought was his friend
> (whom he thought his friend)

[In spoken English and fictional dialogue, it is acceptable to say (or write), "The man that I spoke to...." In formal writing, it should be, "The man to whom I spoke...." See "who / whom" in Usage, and "Who, That?" in the Rogue's Gallery.]

Worth while. Overworked as a term of vague approval and (with *not*) of disapproval. Strictly applicable only to actions: *Is it worth while to telegraph?*

> His books are not worth while.

> His books are not worth reading
> (not worth one's while to read; do not repay reading).

The use of *worth while* before a noun ("a worth while story") is indefensible.

[*Worth while*: Now, of course, usually one word.]

Would. A conditional statement in the first person requires *should*, not *would*.

> I should not have succeeded without his help.

The equivalent of *shall* in indirect quotation after a verb in the past tense is *should*, not *would*.

> He predicted that before long we should have a great surprise.

[*Should*, here, mirrors Strunk's use of *shall*; *would* is now acceptable. In the second example, we would now say something like, "...before long, we would be very surprised."]

To express habitual or repeated action, the past tense, without *would*, is usually sufficient, and from its brevity, more emphatic.

> Once a year he would visit the old mansion.
> Once a year he visited the old mansion.

[For establishing mood, say, in fiction, the first is acceptable.]

VI. Words Often Misspelled

[Strunk's list of words is supplemented by those from the annotator.]

accidentally
accommodate
acronym
advice
advise
affect (verb)
analogous
anomaly
apocalyptic
beginning
believe
benefit
buses (pl. of bus)
buss (elect. term)
cacophony
census
challenge
coeval
colossal
commitment
committed
committee
commonsensical
congeries
consensus
co-opt
corroborate
cozy
criticize
deceive
décor
definite
describe
despise
develop
dichotomy
diphtheria

diphthong
disappoint
duel
ecstasy
effect
encomium
exhilarate
existence
expatriate
extant
fiery
formerly
gauge
genealogy
guerrilla
harass, harassment
heartrending
hemorrhage
hemorrhoid
highfalutin
humorous
hypocrisy
idiosyncrasy
immediately
impresario
inasmuch (as)
incidentally
iridescent
latter
lead
led
loose
lose
magisterial
marriage
memento
mischief

mischievous
misogynist
mnemonic
murmur
necessary
nitpick
nitwit
nuclear
obfuscate
occurred
ophthalmology
parallel
paraphernalia
passagework (music)
peripheral
perquisite
persevere, perseverance
perspicacious
perspicacity
phenomenon
Philip
Phillips (screwdriver)
phony
playwright
pore over (books)
pour (liquids)
possessive
precede, preceding
prejudice
prerequisite
prerogative
prestigious
principal
principle
privilege

pursue
pyrrhic
questionnaire
quintessence
remunerate
remuneration
repetition
rhinoceros
rhyme
rhythm
rhythmic
ridiculous
rigamarole, rigmarole
rumormonger
sacrilegious
seesaw
seize
separate
shepherd
siege
similar
simile
sobriquet
spontaneity
straightened (made straight)
straitened (distressed)
supersede
tee shirt
too
tragedy
traipse
tries
undoubtedly
until
vacillate

Write *any one, every one, some one, some time* (except the sense of formerly) as two words.

[Time, and with it, style, changes. We now write the examples as one word.]

Write *to-day, to-night, to-morrow* (but not *together*) with hyphen.

[Ditto. We no longer hyphenate these words. See "any more / any-more," in Usage.]

THE END

[OF STRUNK'S TEXT]

USAGE

Being a Compendium of Solecisms and Nervous Tics
That Particularly Irritate the Present Writer
(Along with Some Other Things to Think About)

accents : American spelling has tended increasingly to dispense with accents, but in some words accents provide a strong indication of correct pronunciation, and in others they help preserve the original flavor of the word. The accent in *cliché*, for example, militates against the word's sounding like *kleeche*, and *métier* charmingly preserves the word's French origin. (As does *dénouement*. I am even partial to *café*.) *Résumé* profits from the two accents, and *exposé* and *divorcé* positively require their one. The umlaut in *naïf* is a useful reminder to the reader that the word has two syllables. Some writers, and magazines, preserve *naïve*.

Administration / administration : Referred to generally, lower-case *a* is sufficient (the *administration*, or the *administration* of Barack Obama); when it is named specifically, I much prefer *the Obama Administration*. Collectively, don't thousands upon thousands of hard-working bureaucrats, as well as appointees, deserve a capital *A*?

ad nauseam : *To an extreme or disgusting extent.* Often misspelled *ad nauseum*.

adventurous / adventuresome : It may seem like splitting hairs, but there is a subtle difference. The first means disposed to seek adventure (but not to the point of foolhardiness), the second, given to taking risks. A person who likes trekking in the Himalayas is *adventurous*; a guy who rides his skateboard down stair railings is *adventuresome*.

advisor / adviser : Simply alternate spellings, of course, but there are many instances in which one seems preferable to the other. To me, "presidential *advisers*" looks and feels correct, though I prefer "*advisors* to the President." Preferably, a student would write, "I am going to talk to my thesis *advisor*." The first often seems more pleasing to the eye, as well as more expressive, than the second. And it is more consistent with what such a person might provide: an *advisory*.

aesthetic / esthetic : The first strikes me as more pleasing, more *aesthetic*. But I can live with *esthete* almost as easily as with *aesthete*.

affect / effect : Most often, *affect* is a transitive verb meaning *something that produces an effect* (noun). "Inflation is going to *affect* everyone, and have a severe *effect* on spending patterns." *Effect* can also be a transitive (or causative) verb, however, meaning *to succeed in making or doing something*. "We're going to work hard to *effect* change." Among *affect*'s other meanings are *to adopt a use, style, or manner as your own*, as "she *affects* great sophistication." The first definitions (and their typical usages) are by far the most common.

ahead of / run-up to : In the sense of *before the* (e.g.) *election* and in *the period leading up to* (e.g.) *the war*, voguish shorthand; one can only wait patiently for the phrases to go back *out* of vogue. In a phrase like, "the territory ahead of the platoon's advance," *ahead of* is being asked to do too much work, and is therefore imprecise. Does it modify *territory* or *the platoon's advance*? (Note: *Run-up* has a venerable pedigree, but when used to the exclusion of every other phrase, is still breezy shorthand.)

a.m. / p.m. : I prefer to see them capitalized, with a numeral for the hour: *5 P.M.*

any more / anymore : In the sense of *no longer*, the former was once the preferred usage, but it's not *anymore*. The latter spelling helps distinguish the meaning from that of "I couldn't get *any more* out of him," or "I couldn't think of *any more* convincing reason." There has been a tendency, in American English, to combine (rarely to separate) words. *Some one* and *some day* used to be correct. Not *anymore*. Currently, *smokescreen* is making inroads on *smoke screen*.

all right : Always two words; never *alright*. Small potatoes, I know, but when there's a better and a worse, why not choose the better?

although / though : Especially when a sentence includes a strong sense of *despite the fact that*, a strong contrast between two conditions—and especially a strong aversion—be strong yourself, and write *although*. "*Although* I was afraid of riding on motorcycles, I let myself be persuaded."

appears as if / seems as if : *As if* is pretty strongly implied in *appears* and *seems*. Why not be more elegant—and save a syllable—by writing *appears that, seems that*? *Looks as if* is a different story; cf. *looks as though*.

archaeology / archeology : I much prefer the former, as do magazines like *Biblical Archaeology.*

Asian / Oriental : In the first, *of, from, or relating to Asia*; in the second, *of, from, or relating to the Far East.* It is a mistake (and an offensive one) to call an Asian an "Oriental."

awhile / a while : The first is an adverb, meaning *for a while*; it modifies a verb. The second is a noun, meaning *a* (usually short) *period of time*; it is preceded by a preposition. "Stay *awhile,*" but "Stay with me for *a while.*" "Linger *awhile,*" but "I'll see you in *a while.*" Although there is some over-lap between the usages, the distinction is well worth observing; consisten-cy is inherently pleasing.

back in the day : Why this phrase has supplanted the more graphic *back in the old days,* I will never understand. Change is inevitable, but all change is not progress.

ball park / ballpark : Although the former has been losing ground to the latter for many years, it is worth remembering that we do not write *base-ballpark, themepark, footballfield,* or *hockeyrink.* As a colloquial verb, to *ballpark* a figure is a different story.

based in / based out of : Favorite locutions of sports broadcasters, the for-mer seems iffy, and the latter monstrous. "A softball player *based in* [or *out of*] Houston, Texas": doesn't that just mean she grew up there, and/or currently lives there? If she is a seventeen-year-old player, a game in Michigan might represent her first trip out of the state. What does it mean to say she's *based in* Texas?

basically / finally / actually : Try not to let these words become needless padding. "*Basically,* he's a nice person." Isn't there a better way to say it? "May I have some cornbread?" "*Actually,* we're out of cornbread."

B.C. / A.D. / C.E. : Everyone knows that *B.C.* means "before Christ," and *A.D.* means "anno Domini," *in the year of the Lord,* but what does *C.E.* mean? Simple. *Common Era,* a formulation that shows deference to non-Christians, and non-Christian cultures. (It also connotes *Current Era* and, in a curious self-contradiction, *Christian Era.*) *B.C.E.* is best thought of as *Before the Common Era.* All of these formulations, ironically, occlude, but do not expunge completely, the relevance of the birth of Christ. Life is compromise.

being that / being as : As substitutes for *given that, inasmuch as, since*, or *because*, unforgivable.

believe / may, might : Combining two notions for contingency in one sentence is the latest scourge upon the language. "Authorities believe he may have exited through the rear door." That he *may* have exited (no one knows for sure, though that seems probable) is already contained in the tone of conjecture implicit in *believe*. *May*, in this instance, sticks out even worse than would *might*. Better are: "The authorities believe he exited through the rear door," and "Even the authorities don't know, but he might have exited through the rear door." *The authorities*, incidentally, is a hackneyed expression. When possible, be specific: *the police, the sheriff's office, detectives on the scene*.

boy friend / girl friend : Being conservative in matters of language, I prefer the old way: two words. (Curiously, I have several dictionaries that list *boyfriend* as one word, but *girl friend* as two.) A rule change, unfortunately, may be inevitable.

bring / take : You *bring* something back (from there to here), you *take* something to a destination (from here to there). When describing the act, you don't *bring* a letter to the post office, or *bring* your car to the repair shop; you *take* them. Of course, you do *bring* a salad to the potluck, in the sense of conveying it, along with yourself, to that destination.

British spelling : When possible, cleave to American spellings, not British ones: *traveled, canceled* (not *travelled, cancelled*); *color, rumor, flavor* (not *colour, rumour, flavour*); *focused* (not *focussed*); *gray* (not *grey*); *sizable, judgment* (not *sizeable, judgement*). (In America, does one ever see *judgement day*?) *Glamor* is an acceptable alternative to *glamour*, though the latter is prettier. It took two centuries to create an American literary identity distinct from that of the British; why not honor it?

But, to begin a sentence : Before using *But* to begin a sentence, always consider whether the insertion of *however, although, nevertheless*, and the like, later in the sentence, wouldn't be more graceful.

can't help but : *Help* and *but*, in this formulation, are redundant; they serve the same function. "I cannot *help but* think" is trite and wordy (though epidemic in its pervasiveness). Better to write or say, "I *cannot help* thinking," or "I *cannot but* think...."

Capitol / capital : The first is the (or a) building, the second a place, the most important city of a country or region, usually its seat of government. "The United States *Capitol*, which properly should be spelled with a capital *C*, is in our nation's *capital*."

cease-fire / ceasefire : With *crossfire* leading the way, the omission of the hyphen is becoming increasingly common. (In my lifetime, *bestseller* has replaced *best-seller*, *fundraiser*, *fund-raiser*.) In *high-rise* the hyphen is still preferred, but *highrise* is making inroads.

cement / concrete : One of the ingredients of *concrete* is *cement* (the binder), but unlike *cement*, *concrete* also contains, and is made stronger by, an aggregate of gravel, crushed rocks, or even demolition waste.

center on / center around : The first is very much to be preferred. A controversy may seem to *center around* someone or some thing, but the locution is breezy. Try *revolve around* and, when in doubt, use *center on*.

chaperon / chaperone : Both are correct. I prefer the second spelling, because 1) it encourages the correct pronunciation of the last syllable as *own*, and 2) because *chaperones* were originally female.

clichés : Watch out for, and eschew when possible, hackneyed, overused expressions like *shed light, stem the tide, shrouded in mystery, captured in a photograph, go in quest of, my quest for, in search of* (e.g., the title in the book, *In Search of the Trojan War*), *in terms of, lifestyle, resonate, fill the bill, level (on one level), levels* (as in, *her personality functioned on a number of levels), team*. (Why is it always a *team* of scientists or explorers, never *a group, a small group, a talented group, an assortment, a gathering*?) Also, give thought, and when possible find alternatives to, words that are invariably linked: a*bject poverty, innocent bystander, dangerous precedent, momentous decision.*

collectivities followed by verbs : This is a thorny issue, and often instinct and what is called *notional agreement* must lead the way. In general, the choice of verb depends on whether the emphasis is on the quantity, or on the phenomenon to which the quantity refers. "A small number of guests *was* at the party; a great number of them *were* convinced that the day of reckoning was near." Another handy rule of thumb is: *a number* takes a plural verb, and *the number* a singular. "*A number* of us *are* going to the party; *the number* of people who will be there *is* anyone's guess."

compare to / compare with : The first points to differences, the second to resemblances. "I propose to compare life before the war *to* life after the war." "How does beer compare *with* hard cider?" The same holds true with *comparison to* and *comparison with*, as well as *relationship to* and *relationship with*. "He has a lovely relationship *with* his girl friend." "What is her relationship *to* the folks across town who have the same last name?" In the real world, this distinction, though useful to be aware of, contains a considerable gray area.

compliment / complement : Please take care not to spell it the first way when your meaning is the second.

congeries : A *congeries* is *a collection or assortment, usually of things* (though it can also mean a *piling up of language*), and always takes a singular verb. There is no such thing as a *congerie*.

context : Wildly and thoughtlessly overused, and an indication of real laziness on the part of the writer. What does it mean to "put World War II in *context*"? Isn't "describe what led up to it, and its consequences for society" clearer? Because the reader will probably deduce, from the name of an article or book, what is involved, most of the time *neither* phrase is necessary. The use of *context* has reached plaguesome proportions; therefore it completely lacks distinction or any suggestion of originality. In short, it is a cliché. Try to limit the word to the narrow sense in which Strunk uses it: *the discourse that surrounds a word or phrase under discussion. (Context* derives from Latin, *contextus, connection of words, coherence.*) Has there been a writer in the last thirty years who hasn't declared that he or she was going to put his or her subject "in *context*"? It reminds me of the way all articles about literature used to start with an obligatory reference to T. S. Eliot. The phrase, "establish a *context*," is even more gruesome. When a word has been bludgeoned to death from overuse, common sense dictates that one should stay away from it.

converse / obverse : *Converse* (noun or adjective) refers to a situation, object, or statement that is the reverse of another: "The *converse* opinion holds that...." *Obverse* (noun) means *the other side*, e.g., of a coin or the page of a book: "The copyright information is on the *obverse* of the title page." In logic, an *obverse* denies the opposite of that which a given proposition affirms; the *obverse* of "all A is B" is "no A is not B."

criterion / criteria : *Criteria* is still, properly, the plural of *criterion*, and not itself plural. The same goes for *phenomena* and *phenomenon*.

currently / presently : In the sense of happening at the present time, *currently* is often more precise (therefore more pleasing) than *presently*. "He is *currently* teaching at Haverford College." *Presently* is best preserved for its meaning, *in a little while, soon.* "I will return *presently*."

desert / dessert : I have tripped over these spellings my entire life. The first, of course, means *dry, barren, sandy or gravelly land*, the second the *(usually) sweet final course of a meal*. The spellings are counter-intuitive because the verb, *desert (to abandon a cause, person, or military unit)*, is pronounced the same as the noun, *dessert*, namely, *dee-ZERT*. I like parallelism and consistency in language, but often there isn't much; properly, we write *headache*, but not *stomachache*.

discrete / discreet : The first means *individually separate and distinct*, the second, *careful and circumspect in speech or action*; also, *intentionally unobtrusive*. "She is very *discreet* in the way she keeps her relationships *discrete*." Often confused.

dissociate / disassociate : Both are correct. Similarly, *recur* and *reoccur*.

dived / dove : Past tense of *dive*; both are correct. Similarly, *strived, strove*.

drug store / drugstore : I prefer two words, to parallel *book store* and *hardware store*. (Is there any such thing as a *hardwarestore*?) I concede, however, that times are changing.

duct tape / duck tape : Although the first spelling more accurately describes the kind of use to which the tape is put, nowadays, *duct tape* in fact began life as *duck tape*, which was a tape developed by the Army during World War II to wrap, and keep watertight, the lids of ammunition boxes. The tape was so called because it shed water like a duck. A passing curiosity.

due to / owing to : They are synonymous in meaning *because of, attributable to*. "*Due to* circumstances beyond our control," "*Due to* bad weather...." *Owing to*, however, is often more subtle and elegant. "He was late *due to* a flat tire" is lame; "*owing to* a flat tire," by its increased subtlety, doesn't trivialize the problem, but allows—even encourages—one to imagine the frustration and disappointment involved. "*Owing to* her fear of snakes" is simply more dramatic, more expressive, than "*Due to* her fear of snakes." The potential flatness of *due to* is epitomized in the rather windy phrase, *due to the fact that*.

duffel bag / duffle bag : Both are correct, but what is *duffel*, or *duffle*? Not surprisingly, *duffel*, or *duffel*, is *transportable personal belongings, equipment* (often *camping equipment), and supplies.* (It is also a coarse woolen material.) The word comes from *Duffel*, a town in Belgium.

each other / one another : Some usagists prefer *each other* when only two persons, animals, or things are involved, but I find "They're very fond of *each other*" less elegant than "They're very fond of *one another.*" Any time I hear energy moving back and forth from one person to another, I hear *one another*: "They're very affectionate with *one another.*" When more than two people are involved, it is always *one another.* "All the patients are very kind to *one another.*"

Earth / earth : *Earth* is preferable when the planet is being named *as* a planet (cf. *Saturn* and *Jupiter*); *earth* refers to *the soil, the ground, the land on which we stand, the world we inhabit.* Lower-case *earth* should be used in phrases like, "What on earth was he thinking?" When *globe* is being used as a synonym for Earth, some instances seem to benefit from capital *G*. "I have traveled the *globe*," but "the question of food security around the *Globe*...." There is considerable latitude; *the earth* for example, can also name the planet.

emigrate / immigrate : A distinction worth preserving. One *emigrates from* (leaves) one country, and *immigrates to* (enters) another.

end result : Preceding *result* with *end*, is always tempting, but especially in formal writing, is redundant. Similarly, give consideration to *past history, general consensus, future plans, free gift.*

ensure / insure : To me, *ensure* is far more elegant than its weaker synonym, which has its own distinct meaning and therefore can be ambiguous. When a magazine wants to "*insure* continuous service," does it buy insurance for its truck drivers? No, it is going to do everything in its power to see (to *ensure*) that service continues.

etc. : Except at the end of sentences, always followed by a comma. In formal writing it should be avoided; many alternatives, such as *and the like, and so forth*, or *among others*, are available.

euphemisms : Euphemisms are words or phrases people appeal to when they will do anything to avoid calling something what it is. *Downsizing* was once a euphemism for *heartlessly firing people and cutting back operations,* but the reality of a worldwide recession has exposed it for the cynicism it was, and obliterated it from common parlance. Coincidentally, CEOs no longer—or rarely—take *missteps*, businesses no longer *falter*, and markets no longer *stumble*; dire economic realities have supplanted those niceties, and raised the ante. (Cf. market *correction*.). While euphemisms are often inescapable for reasons of tact (what are you going to say when the ninety-four-year-old lady asks you how you like her hat?), ordinary (unreflective) language is so full of *egregious* euphemisms that it would take all day to list them.

factors, a combination of : Everywhere used breezily and imprecisely. Strictly speaking, *factors* don't *combine*. Avoid "a combination of factors" in favor of "several factors contributed to."

farther / further : The first refers to *physical distance* ("I couldn't walk another step *farther*"), the second to *time, degree, or quantity* ("I'm going to pursue the question *further*"). Commonly confused.

field, in the : When possible, find a less pseudo-scientific way to say *not in the office, but working outside.*

flammable / inflammable : They mean the same thing. Signs on trucks carrying dangerous chemicals say *Flammable*, because *Inflammable* might be construed as *not flammable*. (Cf. *habitable* and *inhabitable*.)

flotsam / jetsam : Linking them (*flotsam and jetsam*) subtly retains the distinction between *debris that is* (floating) *in the water for no apparent reason*, and *debris, including cargo, that has purposely been thrown overboard* (jettisoned).

fly to / fly into : The second is yet another gilding of the lily. "I am *flying into* New York": I am not a person who waits in line like everyone else, takes his shoes off at the security clearance, sits for an hour with the company magazine while the airplane waits to take off—I am not trying to *fly to* New York—I am descending from the heavens in a magical conveyance, I am *flying into* New York.

fun : How did the noun, *fun*, get turned into a breezy, catch-all adjective? "It's going to be a *fun* and relaxed evening." Isn't there always a better, less mindless word, one with a little meat on its bones?

gantlet / gauntlet : In yet another case of ordinary usage forcing a change in meaning, the two words are now more or less interchangeable. It is useful to remember, however, that *gantlet* has its origins in roots meaning *street, lane, course,* and *running* (a *gantlet* is also a stretch of railroad track where two sets of tracks overlap), whereas the etymology of *gauntlet* can be traced to *glove.* Until not so very long ago, one would properly have said, "run the *gantlet*" (*run between two lines of persons armed with weapons*), and "throw down the *gauntlet*" (or *issue a challenge*). Now *gauntlet* serves in both meanings.

God / god : When one is not affirming faith in a particular creed or religion, and especially when hinting or suggesting that one is *not* so affirming, *god* is permissible. A specifically religious text, of course, would take *God.*

going forward : Another buzz-phrase of the moment. What's wrong with the kinder, gentler *in the future,* or *in the days ahead?*

Google / google : As a verb, the latter is not quite ready for prime time. Although it is a very useful word, graphic and precise, and even though, like *e-mail, blog,* and *website* (I write *Web site*), it will almost certainly enter the dictionary eventually, it has not, at present, earned its way in. Thanks to computers and *cyberspace,* a word that *has* earned "dictionary rights," an entire new vocabulary is forming around traditional usage; for the moment, however, a careful writer would write: "I searched for it on Google." (Incidentally, *jeep,* from *gp, general purpose vehicle popular during World War II,* entered the language fairly soon after the war was over. Some words have all the luck.) FYI, a *googol* is the numeral 1 followed by a hundred zeros.

got / gotten : When possible, resist the thoughtless temptation to sound British, and use the past participle, *gotten.* "He had gotten [not *got*] involved with some very unsavory people." "A party was *gotten* [not *got*] up for him to celebrate his promotion."

grow the business : A phrase both pompous and mindless; didn't God give us the word, *expand?* Instead of using *grow* as a buzzword, why not say "increase the size [whether of employees or production] of the business"?

hard / difficult : In the sense of *not easy,* they are *almost* synonyms. *Hard* is more informal, and *difficult* implies a greater degree of physical skill or mental ingenuity: "a *difficult* task." "It's *hard* to find cheap apartments, these days" is acceptable, but "ending this charade is going to be *hard*" is much less so. In the second case, *difficult* would have been preferable.

harebrained / hairbrained : The first is the most common, therefore preferable. Hares were thought to have small brains, and/or little sense.

had / would have : "If he *would have* gotten here on time...." Monstrous. Be correct, and say, "If he *had* gotten here...." *Would have*, in this conditional sense, is *never* correct.

her and I / she and I : Pronouns must be used in their correct cases, which can usually be determined by dividing up the sentence in question. "*Her* and *I* are going to the movies"? No. *She* is going to the movies. *I* am going to the movies. Therefore, "*She* and *I* are going to the movies." "The movie appealed to *her* and *I*"? No. The movie appealed to *her*. The movie appealed to *me*. Therefore, "The movie appealed (both) to *her* and (to) *me*."

he'd / she'd : These contractions are among the latest, most thoughtless nervous tics and, what's more, grating to the ear. "Ever since *he'd* left the woods, knowing *he'd* failed to get a shot, *he'd* had a premonition that the deer *he'd* tracked would exact the kind of revenge *he'd* long feared." What's wrong with *he had, she had*?

his, hers / their : Partly owing to (the valuable work of) the women's move-ment, people have become self-conscious about using the possessive ad-jective *his* in sentences like, "Each visitor should leave *his* shoes by the door." Though the practice has a long history, substituting the gender-neutral *their* for *his* ("Each person should leave *their* shoes") grates in my ears, as does "A person who thinks *they* are always right"; being old-fashioned, I still want the number of the pronoun to agree with its antecedent. In the example, one could say, "Each visitor must leave *his or her* shoes," but that seems too wordy for such a small thought, especially when the locution must be repeated. (I consider it infinitely more preferable than *their*, however.) The easiest thing to do is usually to rephrase the sentence: "Visitors should leave their shoes...." A writer with good style who has gently established a precedent can even add charm by writing, e.g., "To each *her* own." I would as soon be shot as write a sentence like the following (from a recent magazine): "No Indian wants to let go of *their* gold." On the subject of number agreement, remember, *people* don't have a chip on their *shoulder*. Collectively they have more than one shoulder, so people have chips on their *shoulders*. I recently gave up in disgust on a how-to book because the author kept referring to "helping people improve their mind." Do *people* have a *mind*? Improvement begins at home, yes? See "Some Things We Collectively Have More Than One Of" in the Rogue's Gallery.

historical / historic : *Historical* means what existed in the past: "The *historical* record shows many instances of...." *Historic* means what was famous or important in history: "The day the Declaration of Independence was signed was a *historic* one." "It was a *historic* moment when we broke ground for the new *Historical* Society." Whether to use *a* or *an* before *historic* is a murky question. In general, words that begin with vowel sounds take *an* (*an amalgamation, an honor*); words that begin with consonants take *a* (*a book, a giraffe*). Americans tend to hear the *hiss* in *historic*, so usually say *a historic*; the Brits would more likely say *an historic*. You will not be shot for saying *an historic*. Cf. *a huge* ship, *a hotel*, in *a hurry*, but *an hour, an herb, an honest* person.

hitherto / thereafter : Most of the time, these seem to me prissy, and slightly mannered. I prefer *up until now*, and *after that*, or *afterward*. On the other hand, *thereafter* is perfectly appropriate in the colloquialisms that mean life after death: *the sweet hereafter, the sweet thereafter*. Other old-fashioned words that should be used sparingly are *theretofore, hereinafter, thereinafter, thence, hence, whence, wither,* and *thither*.

hoard / horde : When you *hoard* (*collect, gather up*) enough stuff and hide it away, you have your personal *hoard*. A *horde* (*a large number of people, animals, or insects*) will sometimes *horde* (*live or move together*). "I've heard that there are *hordes* of theatergoers who *hoard* their old *Playbills*."

hometown / backyard : Until recently, most dictionaries did not consider these to be words. Where did this mania for splicing words together come from? *Backyard, backseat, nametag, prizewinner*.... It seems natural and inevitable that *cell phone* will become *cellphone* (to parallel *telephone*), *best seller, bestseller, smoke screen, smokescreen, health-care* (as an adjective), *healthcare, fund-raising, fundraising*, and I suppose we have to live with *chatrooms* and *newsgroups*. But *home town* is a phrase with such poignant associations that we ought to try to preserve its pronunciation as "home *town*," not "*home*town." The look of *taillight*, although it parallels *headlight*, still trips me up. I have seen, in consecutive sentences, *backyard* and *front yard*, which is just plain silly. I have even seen, as one word, *dominolike, grenadelike, shelllike* (three *l*'s in a row), *arenalike, herpeslike, cabdrivers*, and *machinegunbattle*. (Do we write *automobiledrivers*?) The tendency for compression, in American English, is strong, but we should not let words force their way into the language as a result of carelessness and ignorance. Are we on our way to *trafficticket, computermonitor* and *gasstationattendant*? We need to remember that our objective is to write and speak good English, not good German. See "Whomakes Upthese Compouhndwords" in the Rogue's Gallery.

hopefully : Means *in a hopeful frame of mind.* Strictly speaking, it is not synonymous with *I hope,* or *it is to be hoped.* "*Hopefully* we'll go to the World Series." We'll go to the World Series in a spirit of hope? Yes. I (or we, or they, or the gods) hope we'll go to the World Series? No. There are those who argue that *hopefully* is syntactically the same as *thankfully, mercifully,* and *regrettably,* but hope is such a strong emotion that it seems a shame to slight it with the breezy, floating, unfocused *hopefully.* Here is the more correct usage: "Once Pettite spoke hopefully of retaining [his and Roger Clemens's] friendship."

however / though : *However* is a perfectly good word, but apparently in an attempt to appear casual and folksy (and, perish the thought, make no unnecessary demands upon the reader), writers have everywhere taken to substituting *though.* "She wouldn't drive at the speed he recommended, *though.*" Awful. Let's hear it for a revival of *however.*

iced tea / ice tea : In formal writing, the first is proper; in spoken English, the second passes muster: the *d* is implied aurally. English can be capricious and inconsistent; cf. *ice cream, ice water.*

incident / incidents : It is distressing to have to include this entry, but at a time when one still hears broadcasters saying "incidentces," a reminder is necessary that the plural of *incident* is *incidents.*

indeed / extremely : *Indeed,* to end a sentence, is a British import, so please be careful about using it, much less overusing it. Why write "It was a well-played game, and a fitting end to the season *indeed,*" when "It was an *extremely* [or a *very*] well-played game, and a fitting end..." is available, and avoids possible affectation. To my ear, "The future is exciting indeed" is a sentence appropriate to a feel-good speech; otherwise I would stick to "The future promises to be exciting."

in terms of : Usually, needless padding, a lazy phrase indicative of lazy thinking. "*In terms of* quantity, it was quite substantial."

-ize / -ise : As a verb suffix, most American spelling (unlike British) takes *-ize: patronize, pasteurize, agonize, hospitalize, systematize.* (British would be *patronise, pasteurise,* etc.) Exceptions occur when *-ise* is not a suffix, but intrinsic to the root word: *devise, surmise, advertise, improvise, compromise.*

it's / its : As with *incidentces* for *incidents*, it's distressing to have to include this distinction, but the mistake associated with it is all too common. *It's* is a contraction for *it is* and *it has*; *its* is a possessive adjective modifying a noun or object of an action. "*It's* natural for a dog to think well of *its* owner."

kudos / kudo : From the Greek word for *glory*, or *renown*. In English it has evolved to mean *praise*, or *acclaim*. It is only rarely seen in its singular form.

lay / lie : *Lay* (except when the past tense of *lie*) is transitive, or causative (roughly, something acts on something else), *lie*, intransitive (the verb has no object or referent outside itself). "I'm going to *lay* new brick in the patio," but "I'm going to *lie* down." Except to reward thoughtlessness, there is no advantage in confusing them.

lectern / podium : One stands *at* a lectern (*a stand that holds a text, notes, or microphone*) while standing *on* a podium, or dais (*a raised platform*). Although there is some overlap, by observing the distinction one avoids startling images like, "He gripped the podium."

like / as : In the distinction under consideration, *like* is a preposition, *as* is a subordinate conjunction. "*Like* I said" may be a common locution, but "*As* I said" is correct, and always preferable in formal speech and writing. Correct: "He played *like* a pro, *as* I hoped he would." "He played well, *like* his brother"? No. "He played well, *as* did his brother"? Yes.

likely / probably : Using the former to mean the latter is theoretically correct, but to this writer's ear, very irritating. "It will *likely* rain tomorrow." Not for me, it won't. No, "It will *probably* rain tomorrow." "Rain, tomorrow, may be *likely* (or probable)," but *likely* in a headline like the following seems both breezy and limp. "Oil Will Likely Not Be Contained Until Fall." Adding a qualifier before *likely* makes it seem less offensive: "It will *very likely* rain tomorrow."

lit / lighted : Properly, *lit* is the past tense of the verb, *light*: "He *lit* his pipe." In descriptive, adjectival use, *lighted* is to be preferred: "a well-*lighted* room." Not for nothing did Hemingway entitle his story, "A Clean, Well-*Lighted* Place"; "A Clean, Well-*Lit* Place" would have been lame.

literally : When something is not the case in fact, don't use the adverb *literally*. Do not write, "He was *literally* dead from exhaustion" (unless he *was* dead), or "They *literally* wiped out the other team" (unless they *did* massacre everyone on the other team).

long-lived : The adjective carries more color, more weight, if *lived* is pronounced to rhyme with *dived* (as in, "he *dived* off the pier"). One can also add distinction to one's speech by pronouncing *often* with a soft *t*, making it rhyme with *soften*.

lustre / luster : Even if, strictly speaking, it is British, the first is so much prettier. The second always reminds me of *a person who lusts*.

manner / manor : Many of us are born to the former, few of us to the latter. In *Hamlet*, "to the manner born" has the sense, *accustomed to a practice since birth*. As *manner* and *manor* are pronounced the same way, it was almost inevitable that the second would begin substituting for the first. Colloquially, *manor* is acceptable; the change of meaning even has its charm. Strictly speaking, however, it's *manner*.

may / might : In the present tense, they're fairly straightforward. "We *may* [or *might*] go to the party": *may* suggests a greater degree of probability than *might*. Even here, however, as improbable as it may seem, *may* connotes a granting of permission. "Mom, can we go to the party?" "Yes, you *may* go to the party." (It's the old distinction, "Can you drive my car? Yes. *May* you drive my car? No.") The past tense is trickier. In sports-speak, we constantly hear sentences like, "If he makes the play at second, that run *may* not have scored." This is monstrous. The past tense of *may* is *might*. Leaving aside this announcer's inability to use the subjunctive (*q.v.*), "If he *had made* the play...," he should properly have said, "the run *might* not have scored." Actions completed in the past always take *might* and *might not*. But now we enter a gray area. "They *may* have felt they were in danger." Well, they may *still* feel they were in danger: it's a conjecture, not a statement about something that's past, over and done with. You rush your sister to the hospital; the doctor says, "By not helping, the policeman *may* have made matters worse." Again, it's a conjecture about an ongoing situation, not a statement about a past action. For the rest, especially when referring to something that proved to be contrary to fact, always use *might*: "He *might* have brought his own tools and, if you ask me, he *might* have done a better job." "If the Confederacy had had a larger industrial base, it *might* have won the war." See " 'Might' Makes Right" in the Rogue's Gallery.

me / myself : Most of the time, *myself* is nothing more than a self-important, gilding-of-the-lily substitute for *I* or *me*. "Michelle and *my-*

self....." What's wrong with "Michelle and *I*," or ["Something may happen to] Michelle and *me*"? Similarly with *yourself.* "Before long, I intend to invite Barbara and *yourself* to dinner." What's wrong with *you*?

meanwhile / meantime : Close, but not identical. *Meanwhile* is usually an adverb modifying a verb, *meantime* a noun. "*Meanwhile*, we'll have to wait. In the *meantime*, we can do some much-needed preparation." Because the distinction is so pretty, *in the meanwhile* (though theoretically correct) should probably be avoided.

metaphor / simile / synecdoche : A *metaphor* is simply an understanding of one thing in terms of another, or by analogy. "Until Mrs. Caldwell entered, the classroom was a restless beehive." A *simile* is a kind of weaker metaphor that doesn't say one thing *is* another thing, but is *like* another thing (similes usually include *like* or *as*). "In the final round, he fought *like* a crazed animal." A *synecdoche* (pronounced *si-nek-duh-kee*) uses a part, in the manner of a catch-phrase, to stand, or stand in, for the whole, or the whole for a part. "He applied his John Hancock." "The White House said today...." "Washington has expressed concern...."

meteorologist : It's a matter of personal taste, but this strikes me as a fancy word for a type of person whose needlessly elaborate predictions are wrong about 50 percent of the time. The nineteenth-century term, *weather prophet*, was both more charming and more accurate. Alternatives are *weather forecaster*, which literally captures the nature of the function, and *weatherman* or *weatherperson*.

neither / nor : Notional agreement (roughly, the overall sense and intention of a sentence, rather than strict grammar) sometimes permits *neither...or* followed by a plural verb, especially when more than two clauses are involved: "*Neither* armies, weaponry, *or* violence of any kind *are* sanctioned." In most cases, I prefer *nor*, and a singular verb: "*Neither* he *nor* I *has* the correct tool." Cf. "Neither snow *nor* rain *nor* heat *nor* gloom of night keeps these courageous couriers from the swift completion of their appointed rounds" (Herodotus). As a general rule, one can never go wrong with stricter, rather than looser, usage.

nevertheless / nonetheless : Commonly reckoned synonyms, but one is often preferable to the other. "Many people cheat on their taxes; *nonetheless*, it's wrong." To my ear, *nevertheless* would be better. (An alternative would be, "it's wrong, however.") As the last word of a sentence, *nevertheless* often seems preferable to *nonetheless*. "I know it's snowing, and I'm late, but I'm going to the party *nevertheless.*" I like the overtones of a time element in *nevertheless.*

newspapers, names of : *The New York Times* or the New York *Times?* Whatever the technicalities, the former is certainly easier on the eye than the latter; besides, we would not write: the Wall Street *Journal.* The *The* before newspaper names can also be capitalized: *The Burlington Free Press.* On the other hand, "The *Burlington Free Press* reported...."

none : Takes both singular and plural verbs. "Among the various possibilities, none *seems* exactly right." "None of the solutions we were hoping for *were* available to us."

noplace / anyplace / someplace / everyplace : All are currently acceptable.

nuclear : pronounced *noo-clee-er,* not *noo-kew-ler.*

often : In refined and thoughtful speech, the word is pronounced with a soft *t,* and rhymes with *soften.* That, at least is *my* practice.

okay / O.K. : The first is preferable. In writing, the capital letters, and extra periods, slow sentences down.

only : An adverb that is more than ever, nowadays, placed in the wrong relation to its verb. This is not so bad in spoken speech (though even here it bothers me), but in formal writing it is lamentable. "He *only* believes the moon is made of green cheese because he's misinformed" is much less elegant than "He believes the moon is made of green cheese *only* because he's misinformed." Sometimes the placement of *only* in a sentence is absolutely critical to the sentence's meaning: "The doctor *only* examined the children" (he examined them, and that's all he did). "The doctor examined *only* the children" (he didn't examine the adults). See "If Only...." in the Rogue's Gallery.

over time : A cliché which, when possible, should be avoided; instead, use *gradually, eventually, slowly.* "[Something] will, *in time,* prove its value" is another alternative.

patron / customer : At a hotel or restaurant, one is a *patron*; at a shoe store, one is a *customer.* Those who think of themselves as *customers* in restaurants probably will not take umbrage when, after asking a waiter or waitress whether a certain dish looks delectable, s/he says, brightly: "Oh, yes, I've *sold* six or seven of those tonight!" Do waiters and waitresses *sell* things?

percent / per cent : I much prefer the first form, and I prefer to precede the single word with a numeral. In the phrase, "only twelve percent of the people questioned said...," *twelve percent* tends not to stand out, and to register; *12 percent* is much more graphic. When many percentages are listed, the problem gets worse. Of course, *12%* is a possibility, but especially in the company of many percentages, should probably be restricted to technical writing.

persons / people : *Persons* is preferable to *people* when a group of individuals is being singled out for a remarkable or noteworthy belief, trait, or characteristic. "In New Orleans there were a great many free *persons* of color" (not "free *people* of color"). The seriousness or solemnity of the thought might also dictate the use of *person*. "When these *persons* broke out of the detention camp...." *People* implies *many*; *persons*, *individuals*.

piece : As applied to a magazine article, use sparingly lest it sound like an affected, in-group word.

point in time / time period : *At this point in time*: needlessly wordy. Try *at this point*, or *at this time*; for the second, *at this time, during this period*.

possessives modifying gerunds : Gerunds are words ending in -*ing* that have the function of nouns: "*swimming* is fun," and (with linking words) "*being* healthy is preferable to *being* sick." In most cases, the nouns or pronouns that precede gerunds should be possessive. "The result of *him* being late..." is less elegant than "The result of *his* being late...." "The *vaccine* proving itself effective was a great relief" is less elegant than "the *vaccine's* proving itself...." "Do you mind *me* taking your umbrella?" is less elegant than "Do you mind *my* taking your umbrella?" The issue gets complicated, however, because some phrases simply do not sound right with the possessive, e.g., "The result of several *men's* being late...." Here, *men* is acceptable. Other exceptions (and grammar is full of exceptions) occur when the noun ends in *s*: "without the *parties* having any choice" (no apostrophe) and, most often, when the emphasis seems to be on the subject, not the action: "I couldn't stand to see *him* getting that interception" (the emphasis is on *him*, not *getting*). As Strunk says, "By using the possessive, the writer will always [or at least usually] be on the safe side."

pre- / re- / co- : As prefixes, should one hyphenate or not? It depends. More and more words are dropping the hyphen (e.g., *reenter, recopy, rediscover*), but there is a limit to how much visual ambiguity can be tolerated. *Co-op* (but not *cooperative*) requires a hyphen so as not to lead to confusion with *coop, co-opt* without a hyphen leads to *coopt*, and *co-wrote* without a hyphen produces the startling, *cowrote*.

premise / premises : In common usage, a *premise* is *a proposition that forms the basis of an argument, or from which a conclusion is drawn.* "He worked on the *premise* that...." In its most common form, *premises* means *a piece of land and the buildings on it, or a part of a building, especially when used for commercial purposes.* When one is in a restaurant, one is "on the *premises*," not "on the *premise*."

President / president : I prefer the former because, even when the President isn't named, I believe the office warrants the respect that the capital *P* provides. I also write *Vice President* (in the Constitution, the title is hyphenated), and *Secretary of State*.

primer / primer : One, pronounced *primmer*, refers to a small book used for instruction, usually in reading skills. The other, pronounced *prymer*, refers to something used to start a process (as a verb, one *primes* a well, or *primes* explosives); as a noun, *primer* is a first coat of paint, or other material.

prone / supine / prostrate : When used to describe a person on the ground, *prone* generally means *lying face down*, and *supine, lying face up.* There are many ways to blur the distinction, but inasmuch as we have both words, why not use them? *Prostrate* can mean either *lying prone, stretched out horizontally,* or *lying face downward in worship or submission.*

proved / proven : Contemporary writers, for no good reason, seem to be shying away from *proven* as a past participle for *prove.* That's unfortunate, because *proven* is often more elegant than *proved.* ("It has been *proven* that....") In precise, either/or matters like those investigated by science or mathematics, *proved* makes the most sense ("that the number 12 has four factors has been *proved*"), but *proven* is better in sentences like, "Vitamin C's effectiveness in preventing scurvy has been *proven*." As an adjective, *proven* is the safest choice ("she is a person of *proven* ability"); it is *de rigueur* in the phrase, "innocent until *proven* guilty."

rack / wrack : "He felt he must *rack* [*stretch or strain*] his brains to find ways to keep from feeling he was on the *rack* [*instrument of torture*]. To fail, he felt, would be to go to *wrack* [*wreckage*] and ruin."

reason is because, the : I side with those who think the phrase redundant, *because* being implicit in the word *reason*; when possible, I cleave to *the reason that*. "The reason I am late is *that* I had an accident" is so much nicer than "The reason I am late is *because* I had an accident."

regard / regards : You send *regards*, and hold someone in high *regard*, but when you are referring to something, it is in *regard* to, never in *regards* to. (*As regards* is also correct.) *Apropos regardless / irregardless*, there is no such word as *irregardless*; the *ir* in that non-word duplicates the function of *less*.

rock 'n roll / rock and roll : A small matter, but I prefer the first; *rock 'n' roll* is another possibility.

self-conscious : It's a pity that the still-mandatory hyphen leads to combinations like *unself-conscious*, because the *un* seems to refer more to *self* than to *conscious*. But for the moment, there's no way around it.

skeptic / sceptic : The first is the preferred American spelling, the second the preferred British.

sneaked / snuck : The past, and past participle, of *sneak* is *sneaked*, though *snuck* is inexorably forcing itself into the language, and may eventually take over. Will *leaked* then become *luck*, and *peaked*, *puck*? In formal writing, always *sneaked*.

so far as / as far as : In the sense provided in the following examples, *so far as* is often more graphic, and more expressive, than *as far as*. "*So far as* getting there on time, I don't think the weather will be a factor." "*So far as* the evidence may be believed...." *So far as* has a bit of panache that *as far as* lacks.

species / specie : It is best to use the first in its sense of *category*, and give it a singular verb ("The *species is* dying out"), and reserve the latter for its meaning, *money in the form of coins*.

split infinitives : "He agreed to also send a check." Properly, "He agreed also to send a check." (Best of all, "He also agreed to send a check.") "He wanted to both thank Jane and shower her with compliments." Properly, "He wanted both to thank Jane and...." In general, except when the ear dictates otherwise, any unnecessary separation of verbs from the subjects they delineate should be avoided, e.g., "The students are, on the whole, very enthusiastic." Such separation often requires the insertion of commas where few, or even none, would have been necessary. "Having begun as an American playwright, O'Neill had become, in the end, an Irish one." Better, "Having begun as an American playwright, in the end O'Neill had become an Irish one." (Two fewer commas.) "Rearranging facts or chronology was, in his view, permissible." Better, "Rearranging facts or chronology, in his view, was permissible." (One less comma.) "Rearranging facts or chronology in his view was...." (*No* commas.) "The implication is, nevertheless, that...." Better, "The implication, nevertheless, is that...." "Coming out of a state of nature, man had, by making a compact, vested power in the government." Better, "Coming out of a state of nature, man, by making a compact, had vested...." These skewed verb forms lead to writing that is ungainly and inelegant. From a recent novel: "The trouble was that there had never, in the past, been a time exactly like this." And, "Life did, after all, have to go on." The syntax in question has become such a pestilence that it warrants another example or two. "He would, upon receipt of his check, agree to review the whole situation." Better, "Upon receipt of his check, he would agree...." "White men with modest capital, on the labor of blacks, convert the wilderness to...." "The destinies of black men and women were, even more than those of whites, a consequence of...." Using herky-jerky syntax is apparently something writers resort to, consciously or unconsciously, to make sentences seem like they have more weight than they do. See "Let's-Chop-the-Sentence-Up," and "Split Ends and Split Infinitives," in the Rogue's Gallery.

stance : Often a lame substitute for *viewpoint, standpoint, attitude, approach, position,* or *sensibility*—and ambiguous to boot. "His poetic *stance*": his position regarding poetry, or a reference to the poetic manner in which he stands?

stationary / stationery : For a few moments, at least, a shopper will probably have to remain *stationary* (immobile) while shopping for *stationery* (writing materials, especially paper) in a *stationery* store.

subjunctive, the : "If I *were* in charge," or "if I *was* in charge"? In refined speech and writing, the first is much to be preferred. The subjunctive (in the sense being considered here) should always be used when the matter being referred to is not a fact, but only contingent, or *possible.* "If he *were* a better golfer," not "If he *was* a better golfer...." I have grown so tired of —and irritated by—hearing on television phrases like, "If I'm the Dallas Cowboys, I gotta believe...," that I wrote a story, "Reginald Used the Subjunctive Today," in which, in a post-apocalyptic setting, quasi-clerical elders try desperately to teach wayward boys the basic elements of good grammar. How much more time does it take to say, "If I *were* the Dallas Cowboys, I *would have to* believe..."—and in the process make one less addition to the dumbing-down of America? "If he *makes* that catch" (referring to a past event)...the assault on the subjunctive, and generally, precision in language, is on us like a tidal wave. See the section on the Subjunctive in the Rogue's Gallery.

such as / such [word] as : *Such as* is a very lazy way to introduce an example, or examples, and *such [word] as* (*such newspapers as*) is worse. "*Such* thorny and persistent problems *as* the tendency of the cable to break" is a mouthful. There are many more stylish ways of phrasing the thought.

that / which : *That* used as a pronoun (not an adjective or conjunction) precedes a phrase that defines what is being referred to (it is *restrictive*), *which* precedes a description or amplification (*which* is *nonrestrictive*). "The house *that* I bought in the country needs a lot of work" (*that* house is the only house in question). "The house I bought in the country, *which* was built in 1810, needs a lot of work" (the *which* clause adds information to the main point). *Which* is usually bracketed with commas, which leads to a convenient mnemonic device: *which*, like *comma*, has five letters. Sometimes sound and sense must serve as guide, however. "Deep plowing in the heartland destroyed many of the grasses *that* for ages had captured moisture and held the land firmly in place." I hear the sentence as "*which*, for ages, had captured...." The pause surrounding a *which* phrase is sometimes suggested by dashes or parentheses. "The house *that* I bought in the country (*which* was built in 1810) needs...." Apparently, in an effort not to put undue pressure on the reader (perish forfend that she should have to slow down for an instant), many writers have gotten into the bad habit of omitting the restrictive pronoun, *that*, sometimes with startling consequences: "The doctor felt her breast needed examination." "Please notice the signs in the lobby have been removed." Are we being asked to notice the signs, or to remember them now that they've been removed? Among haphazard writers, *that* is everywhere making inroads in situations where *who* is much to be preferred. "Bob is a person *that* likes to fish." "He is one of those people *that* loves to eat." Please, whenever possible let's retain our loyalty to *who*. See "That, Who?" in the Rogue's Gallery.

theater / theatre : A reasonable procedure is to use the first to name the place, the second to name the art form. "I was at the *theater* (the building), last night, helping to make plans for next year's *theatre program* (schedule of plays)."

toward / towards : *Toward* is American usage, *towards*, British. Use *toward*. Similarly, *forward* (as an adverb) is preferable to *forwards*.

trouper / trooper : A *trouper* (from *troupe*) is a person who rises to the occasion, and carries on gamely through good times and bad. A *trooper*, typically, is a member of the state police. The latter is sometimes made to stand in for the former.

try and : Acceptable, though *try to* is prettier. "I'm going to *try to* pay him back before June" somehow seems more expressive than "I'm going to *try and* pay him back before June." *Try and* is especially not acceptable when an adverb is involved: "I love going to school, and *try* always *to* be on time."

unconscious / subconscious : When used as nouns in reference to the history and technique of psychoanalysis (and especially in reference to Freud), the first is correct, the second is not. In general usage, *unconscious* and *unconsciously* are often preferable to *subconscious* and *subconsciously*. "He did it *unconsciously*," not *subconsciously*.

underway / under way : Commonly confused. *Underway* is an adjective, as in an *underway* boat, an *underway* refueling. *Under way* has a verbal or an adverbial function, and means *in motion* or *in progress*. "The boat [or game or season or concert] got *under way* right on time."

unique : The only one like it, the only one in its class; *sui generis*. Nothing, nothing, nothing can be *rather* unique, *very* unique, or *extremely* unique. There are plenty of other ways to say that something is special, e.g., *rare*, *unusual*, *distinct*, or *exceptional*. Why not let *unique* retain its discrete, special meaning, its venerable, one-of-a kind pride of place?

until / till / 'til : The first two are much to be preferred (*till*, interestingly, is an older word than *until*). To begin a sentence or clause, *until* is usually best.

used to / use to : Most of the time, the first is the phrase of choice: "He *used to* go to football games all the time." After *did* or *didn't*, however, it gets tricky. Best, probably, is: "He didn't *use to* be like that."

utilize / use : Except in specialized or technical writing, *utilize* is a needless affectation. Why *use* a ten-dollar word (and add syllables) when the twenty-five-cent word is perfectly adequate? Similarly, be mindful of using *commence* when *begin* would do, *demise* when *death* would do, *effectuate* when *effect* would do. Simplify, simplify.

venue : What was originally a legal term is being used more and more loosely, until it is now being *mis*used ("our magazine is a good *venue* in which to publish"). The non-technical, permissible use is: *physical place where something happens, especially an organized event such as a concert, conference, or sports event.* I recently heard a baseball announcer say, "He [the pitcher] looks to first and then to third, but doesn't throw to either *venue*." Please.

verbiage / wording : *Verbiage* means *a superfluity or excess of words, wordiness*, though it can also mean, simply, *diction* or *wording* (concise military *verbiage*). But there are many synonyms for the latter meaning (*speech, language, terminology, wording*); why not save the graphic *verbiage*, with its connotations of disapproval and demurrer, for speech that is excessive, and vaguely (or not so vaguely) offensive?

vexed : Almost invariably, *the vexed question*, or *the vexed issue*, but rarely do people use either phrase in speech. Except when being mischievous or playful, avoid words that you rarely hear spoken. These include *riffle* (in the sense of small waves on water), *scud, scudding, louche, swot, vole*, and *tergiversate*. Unusual words stand out; you don't want your style to *show*.

victuals : Food supplies, provisions. Pronounced *vittles*.

we / us : *We* is the nominative (loosely, the subject) case; cf. *name*. *Us* is the objective case (loosely, that toward which the subject points); cf. *object*. "*We* Americans should learn to write with more precision," but "Learning to write with more precision should be a goal for all of *us* Americans."

whether / whether or not : The second phrase is perfectly acceptable, but the *or not* can often be omitted.

who / whom / whoever / whomever : *Who* has to do with subjects (the person or persons initiating the action), and *whom* with objects (the person or persons acted upon). "*Who* brought all the food?" But, "To *whom* are we indebted for bringing all the food?" Forgetting, for the moment, that it was probably a female who did the work and brought the food, we can make a useful mnemonic by linking *him* and *whom*, which both end in *m*. Then, if we rephrase the sentence, and it clearly takes *him*, we know to use *whom*; if it takes *he*, we use *who*. "*He* brought all the food" yields *who*. "The food, for which we are indebted, was brought by *him*" yields *whom*. (Obviously, *she* and *her* are syntactically equivalent to *he* and *him*, there just isn't a handy mnemonic using those words.) "The prize will go to *whoever* wins the most votes," or "*whomever* wins the most votes"? Here, the last five words are a unit, with a subject (*he* who wins) and an object (votes), so *whoever* is correct. "I will speak to *whoever* I please," or "*whomever* I please"? "I will speak to *him*," so *whomever* is correct. Note that in both cases, the *him-whom* mnemonic works. There is considerable latitude in these usages, and often the final appeal must be to sound, instinct, and common sense; more care will be required in formal writing than in everyday speech.

who's / whose : *Who's* is a contraction for *who is, who has*. *Whose* is a possessive pronoun. "*Who's* going to find out *whose* eyeglasses these are?"

widow / orphan : In printing, a *widow* is the last line of a paragraph when it is carried over to the following page. An *orphan* is the first line of a paragraph when it appears at the *bottom* of a page. Widows are considered more unsightly than orphans; the way to prevent them is to bring *two* lines from the bottom of the previous page to the top of the following page.

widow / widower : *Widow:* the surviving wife. *Widower:* the surviving husband.

wreaked / wrought : It's a shame that writers have taken to shying away from the verb, *wrought*. As an old-fashioned past tense and past participle of *work*, it is often more expressive, and more musical, than *wreaked*. "The hurricane *wrought* considerable havoc on the marina": Here, using *wreaked* results in quite a mouthful. In the rhetorical question, "What hath God wrought," *wrought* has the sense of *fashioned*; as an adjective, the word retains this sense: *wrought* iron.

years of age : Needless padding of the perfectly adequate, *years old*.

yesterday / the previous day : "Yesterday I went to school" is obviously correct. In narrative sentences like "He had learned *yesterday* that she had...," substitute *the previous day*.

USAGE, II

all that / not all that : "The President is *not all that* concerned about the threat of a strike." Lazy, breezy, and slangy. Why not be more precise, and more graphic, by saying "not very," "not greatly," or "not particularly"?

ax / axe : The first is the more common American spelling, the second the more common British.

criteria / criterion : *Criteria* is still, properly, the plural of *criterion*; *criterion*, properly, is not plural, *criteria* not singular. The same goes for *phenomena* and *phenomenon*.

drier / dryer : The first means *more dry*, the second refers to the electrical appliance. One puts one's clothes in a clothes *dryer* (one's hands under a hand *dryer*) in order to dry them, or at least make them *drier*. The distinction is pleasing, though not hard and fast.

flier / flyer : They are identical in all their various meanings. American English prefers the former spelling, British English the latter.

forego / forgo : These are *homophones*, words that are pronounced the same, but have different (in this case, entirely different) meanings. *Forego* means *to precede or come before*; the *fore* in the word indicates the time element. (A *foregone conclusion* is a conclusion that is inevitable.) *Forgo* means *to do without or abstain from, to pass up voluntarily*. "I will *forgo* dessert." But: "Your summary must *forego* the body of your dissertation." Commonly confused.

hanged / hung : Unless the subject is death as punishment or by suicide, *hung* is always correct. "On the day he was *hanged*, a mist *hung* over the courtyard."

hark back / hearken (or **harken**) **back** : *To revert to an earlier topic or circumstance*; also, *listen attentively*. The first of the three spellings is to be preferred.

---

interment / internment : The first refers to the process of burial, the second to the act of detaining people, especially during wartime. An *internship* is what an *intern* serves, who is an apprentice or trainee gaining practical experience.

just deserts / just desserts : Though the second is sometimes irresistible, and carries a pleasing irony, the first is correct: Here, *deserts* is the plural of (the rare and archaic) *desert*, meaning *that which one deserves*.

leaped / leapt : As the past tense and past participle of *leap*, both are correct. Except in colloquial usages like "That movie *creeped* me out," the past tense of *creep* is *crept*.

lend / loan : Traditionally, the first is a verb, the second a noun, but *loan* is increasingly being used to mean *lend*. In figurative uses, *lend* and *lent* are appropriate: Marc Antony did not ask the Romans to *loan* him their ears. Cf.: "The sunset *lent* a beautiful orange glow to the clouds."

less / fewer : Because Strunk's exegesis (*analysis* or *interpretation*) of these two words is rather skimpy (and even somewhat ambiguous), and because there is a very nifty way to differentiate them, I will round out the discussion here. *Fewer* applies to *things that can be counted*: toys, souvenirs, friends, baseballs; *less* applies to *things that cannot be counted*: furniture, paint, air, amounts in the general sense (e.g., time, distance, and money). One might have *less* paint than one needs, but one has *fewer* gallons of paint than one needs. After a trip to Las Vegas, one might have *fewer* dollars than before, but one has *less* money. "If we make *fewer* stops, we can be there in *less* than two hours." "If we had *fewer* chairs in this room, there would be *less* clutter." In a curious (and pleasing) display of common sense, things that can be counted are called *count nouns*; things that cannot be counted are called *mass nouns*. Because they are *mass nouns*, one cannot have *fewer* furniture, *fewer* paint, *fewer* clutter. *Collective nouns* are a subset of *mass nouns*, and denote groups with two or more members: *couple, family, herd, team, committee, faculty,* and the like. In America, collective nouns usually, but not always, take singular verbs: "The corporation *is*," "the faculty *is*"; in England, they more often take plural verbs: "The faculty *are*...." Whether to use a singular or plural verb, with collective nouns, is a function of whether the emphasis is on the group's sense and meaning as a unit, or on its members as individuals. "The couple *is* moving to Idaho," but "The couple *are* going their separate ways." "The family *is* very wealthy," but "The family *are* all avid golfers."

loath / loathe : The first is an adjective, meaning *unwilling, reluctant*, or *averse to*; the second is a verb, meaning *to dislike greatly*. "I am *loath* to tell you how much I *loathe* that man." As an adjective, it is *loathsome*, meaning *disgusting, revolting, repellent*. One may approach a task with fear and *loathing*. Commonly confused.

meager / meagre : Their meanings are identical; the first is simply the preferred American spelling, the latter the British.

mean / median : If the train runs mostly at seventy miles an hour, but occasionally at thirty, its *mean* (average) speed would be closer to seventy than to thirty. If, once it gets going, the train runs as low as thirty, and as high as seventy miles an hour, its *median* (middle, or at-the-center) speed would be fifty: Half its speeds are below fifty, and half are above.

militate / mitigate : *Militate* means *to have a substantial effect, to weigh heavily*, and is usually followed by *against*. "Lack of provisions *militated* against our proceeding farther." *Mitigate* means *to lessen in force, intensity, or severity*. "The judge asked whether there were any reasons for her to *mitigate* the punishment."

moustache / mustache : Both are correct. This writer much prefers the first spelling.

torturous / tortuous : "Whichever road / Or twisted path / The world in its torturous / Logic decides on...." That was the first stanza of a poem of mine, called "Sure Footing at a Snowy Intersection." About two years after I wrote it, I came across the word, *tortuous*. A typo, of course. Absolutely not. *Torturous* means *involving, or causing torture* (a *torturous* treatment); *tortuous* means *twisting, winding, convoluted* (a *tortuous* explanation). The word I wanted was *tortuous*.

whiskey / whisky : If it's made in Scotland, it should be *whisky*: Scotch *whisky*. Most other places, including Ireland and the United States, it's *whiskey*.

LITTLE DOTS AND SQUIGGLY THINGS

Punctuation

, comma : When more than two things are itemized, a comma should follow every item except the last. This use of the *serial comma* always adds clarity, and is *never* out of place. Are not "red, white, and blue" and "this, that, and the other" more graphic than "red, white and blue" and "this, that and the other"? A woeful disregard of this rule is currently pandemic. (An exception is when two adjectives or adjectival phrases clarify or amplify a previous adjective. In the line in Robert Frost's poem, "The woods are lovely, dark and deep," "dark and deep" describe *how* the woods are lovely.) ¶ Commas after *and, yet, but, that,* and *for*: Despite the current obsession with inserting them, they are usually, or at least often, not necessary—in fact are intrusive and out of place. "But, suddenly, all eyes turned away from the intruder." What earthly function do the commas serve, except to dilute the force of *suddenly,* and slow the sentence down? When possible, I try not to bracket with commas conjunctions like *and* and *or.* "It is useful to familiarize oneself with the rules of grammar and, more to the point, observe them in practice": no comma before *and.* I recently saw a sentence in a popular magazine that contained *nine* commas (as well as a dash and an italicized word). All that *in one sentence.* The above notwithstanding, the use of the comma affords a writer wide discretion. It may be used anywhere a (legitimate) pause is indicated, or needs to be encouraged.

; semicolon : Except in lists (or a series of elements) comprised of long phrases, it is best to use no more than one in a given sentence. To mix up rhythms and prevent predictability ("predictability is the death of art," said Roland Barthes), try to avoid the semicolon in consecutive sentences. The British often use semicolons where we would use commas.

: colon : Between the end of one sentence and the beginning of another, when at all possible use a period instead. In many cases, the reader will easily make the connection, that is, will quickly grasp how one element follows from the other. When a complete sentence ends in a colon and is *followed* by a complete sentence, the first word of the second sentence should be capitalized. When a colon sets off a list within a sentence, or the second clause is a brief explanation of the first, the word following the colon should *not* be capitalized.

- hyphen : Usually not necessary between commonly linked words (*intensive care unit, short story writer*), definitely not necessary between words that are always capitalized (*Civil War diaries, New Deal policies*). In addition, hyphens are never necessary after adverbs ending in *ly* (though the British favor them). *Thoroughly modern*: yes. *Thoroughly-modern*: no. Note that there are many phrases in which the use or omission of the hyphen will depend on the flow of the sentence, as in "his gleaming, brand new car," or "the living room rug." *Brand new* and *living room* are often linked, so especially in *living room*, a hyphen is not needed. With *brand new* it might depend on the length of the sentence, and which element within it the writer wishes to emphasize; it's a question of instinct and taste.

— / ( ) dashes and parentheses : Do not use a dash when a semicolon, or even a comma, will suffice, e.g., "I ate an apple—I'm very fond of apples." Just because you're changing gears is no reason compulsively to reach for a dash; semicolons and periods provide perfectly good ways to change gears. Besides, too many dashes keep prose from looking smooth and seamless on the page. (In a book by a college professor, I recently saw nine sets, a total of *eighteen*, dashes on two facing pages.) In the following, the dash serves no real purpose: "The inevitable removal of master from slave was particularly heightened by that crown of Southern evolution—the plantation." Whenever possible, avoid placing a phrase set off by dashes within a phrase or sentence set off by parentheses; similarly, avoid placing a phrase set off by parentheses within a phrase set off by dashes. Keep punctuation to the absolute minimum that is necessary. As William Strunk might have said, "Simplify, simplify, simplify."

' apostrophe : Not to be used with *its* (*q.v.*) as a possessive: "A dog loves *it's* master." The mistake is all too common. Don't use an apostrophe with dates (*1980s* is preferable to *1980's*), or with plurals of abbreviations that have no periods (*CEOs, IPOs, ATMs*, but *Ph.D.'s, M.D.'s*), certainly not to indicate plurals of names (*the Johnson's*). Another way to write dates given in decades, one that's easy on the eye, is *the Eighties*.

italics : Try to avoid italicizing a word, or words, in phrases that are set off by dashes; the dashes already provide emphasis. Italics are rarely necessary in sentences that end with exclamation points; the exclamation point provides the emphasis. Do not overuse italics; most of the time they aren't necessary. In a well-constructed sentence, the emphasis will fall naturally on the word to be emphasized, and the reader will hear that emphasis. (I have read many books by British authors in which italics were not used even once.) It's a matter of taste, but I prefer to see specialized foreign-language imports like *apropos* and *per se* set off in italics. This applies to other words or phrases that have retained their specialized, or foreign flavors, e.g., *nom de plume, coup de grace, idée fixe, a fortiori.* Although there are many other words and phrases that seem not to need italics (*ad hoc, ad infinitum, alma mater*), one can never go wrong by italicizing them.

" quotation marks with other punctuation : Proper American usage is always to place commas and periods *inside* of close-quotation marks, both single and double, but colons and semicolons *outside.* The exception, for periods, is when sentences end with a parenthetical phrase; in this case, the period goes *outside* the parenthesis. (The British place almost everything outside of close-quotes.) Some fine tuning is required when a sentence contains single quotes, and ends with a question mark, or exclamation point. Following is an example from dialogue in a novel: "What do you mean, 'the door hit him on the head'?" ¶ The titles of short stories, short poems, short musical compositions, plays, chapters of books, and radio and television programs take quotation marks. The titles of novels, longer poems (*The Iliad*), and musical compositions (Beethoven's *Fifth Symphony*) take italics. Coleridge's *The Rime of the Ancient Mariner* could take either quotation marks, or italics; italics seem appropriate to the weight and somberness of the poem.

... ellipses : When used to show the omission of words at the beginning of, or within a quote, three dots; at the end of a quote, four. I often add extra space after the fourth dot (the period) in order to avoid visual confusion. "Four score and seven years ago our fathers brought forth a new nation....Now we are engaged in a great civil war....We are met on a great battlefield...." Space, even extra space, after *nation.... war....* and *battlefield....*

? ! question marks / exclamation points : Avoid using them together, as in *?!* . If a sentence is thoughtfully constructed, the reader will hear the exclamatory aspect of a question, and the questioning aspect of an exclamation. Except in casual writing (letters, say), multiple question marks and exclamation points (*??* or *!!*) are *never* warranted.

Simplify, simplify, simplify.

ROGUE'S GALLERY

A Tour of Haphazard Writing in Newspapers and Magazines, And Some Observations About Language

The proof of the pudding, knowing how to speak and write elegantly, is in the eating—the language we actually hear and read—and it seems to me that there is a fair amount of stale pudding around, these days. There are a number of reasons for this. Most important is the gradual decline of language as the heart and soul of Western culture; visual media and other electronic technologies are encroaching, and faster and faster, upon its centrality. This has led to an educational system in which English is no longer taught as rigorously as it once was. Greek and Latin are now specialties, ancient models of fine writing are no longer memorized and emulated, and there is probably not one high school student in a hundred who knows how to diagram a sentence. Verb forms like the subjunctive, once so indicative of precise and subtle thought, are now routinely mutilated on radio and television, and because people hear the mutilations day in and day out, it is no wonder that they don't understand proper usage. Finally, it must be remembered that we are a nation of immigrants. If it's all teachers can do to teach basic English, how can they be expected to teach the pluperfect subjunctive?

The gradual contraction of the print media (fewer and smaller newspapers, fewer publishers, fewer books) naturally has led to budget cuts, and this, in turn, has drastically reduced the number of proficient copy editors. And copy editors used to be the gatekeepers of, and the last line of defense for, the printed word. Nowadays, reporters submit their stories directly from their laptops to newspapers' composing rooms, and authors submit their books on floppy disks, or by e-mail; all rely on computer spell-checkers and syntax programs to point out errors, and fix accidents. If the articles and stories get edited at all, it is by editors who are themselves being swept up in the spread of loose, breezy, and error-filled language. Don't even mention texting....

The ironic thing about taste is that the better one's is, the more things there are to offend it. As I've bristled over the quotes that follow (all taken from current magazines and newspapers), and have dutifully written them down and transcribed them, I've often asked myself: am I being picky? Is this whole activity petty? Am I small-minded, schoolmarmish, and a snit to boot (so to speak)? The reader should know that I don't *like* to criticize, blame, and find fault. But if the thought that I'm a fault-finder irritates me, what irritates me even more is that there is so much fault to find. As I said in the Foreword, grammar and usage are not God-given and immutable; they inevitably go through changes and metamorphoses. I just happen to think that if something works well, and has worked well for a long time, there ought to be a good, convincing, and logical reason to change it. In fact, I could be happy with Black English (*I be, you be, we be, he be, she be, they be*) if that were the way the majority of us were currently playing the game of language. But it's not. We're playing the language game differently, and no one has ever given me a good reason why we shouldn't play the game as well, that is, as elegantly and as beautifully, as possible.

So let's take a little tour of the world of newspaper and magazine English, and examine some of the ingredients that have lately made for some pretty stale pudding. Please: read consecutively, or feel free to browse.

S.P.

Note: The magazines, newspapers, and Web sites from which the following quotations were taken are identified as: *America's Civil War* (*ACW*), *The Boston Globe* (*BG*), *Boston Herald* (*BH*), CNN Online (*CNN*), the *Eagle* (a Vermont newspaper) (*EVT*), ESPN Online (*ESPN*), *Discover* (*D*), *Flight Training* (the magazine of the Aircraft Owners and Pilots Association) (*FT*), *Harper's Magazine* (*H*), London *Telegraph* (*LT*), Major League Baseball Online (*MLB*), *The Nation* (*N*), *New Scientist* (*NS*), *Newsweek* (*NSWK*), *New York Daily News* (*NYDN*), *The New Yorker* (*NYer*), *The New York Review of Books* (*NYR*), *The New York Times* (*NYT*), *New York Times* [Sunday] *Magazine* (*NYTM*), *Smithsonian* (*S*), *USA Today* (*USA*), *Time* (*T*), *Vermont Life* (*VL*), and *The Wall Street Journal* (*WSJ*).

In showing how the following sentences might have been improved, I use "**www**" to mean "what's wrong with?" But first:

Department of You Can't Make This Stuff Up

The qualities William Strunk sought to encourage in language can be summed up by two words: common sense. He hated obfuscation, unnecessary jargon, and anything that might needlessly confuse or mystify the reader. What do you suppose he would have thought of the following?

1) "For all that he encompasses every powerchord and emcee front, stripper swing and ragtime ostinato, he persists in turning that plenitude inward, encoding the very experience of influence. When we listen to his transformations of canonical classical music especially, we are listening to music by listening to listening, as what has to be called Zorn's music, and nothing but Zorn's music, reveals itself in its newness and shocking historicity." *H*

2) "Living as we do in this postmodern age, we have become increasingly interested in the origins of our predecessor, the modern world." *NYR* (Don't you just wake up, every morning, knowing that you live in the "postmodern age," and wondering about what went on in the old days, "the modern world"?)

Now some writing that could have been better, simpler, and more to the point:

Serial Killers

"Warrants for searches conducted this week…authorized federal drug agents and LAPD to seize emails…between the cardiologist, Jackson and Beverly Hills dermatologist…." Are "Jackson and Beverly Hills" the cardiologist or the dermatologist? Why not a simple little comma after *Jackson*? They don't cost much.

Ah, what havoc can be wrought by the omission of our little friend, the serial comma! Listen to the way, *without* the serial comma in the last clause, the following sentence comes crashing to a bumpy end: "It had everything he needed: two single beds—one for himself, the other for his papers—a divan, an overstuffed chair, four gas burners atop a stove he was afraid to ignite, an unsteady card table on which to work and Art Nouveau lamps." *S*

"An adaptation of Margaret Mitchell's thousand-page blockbuster novel, from 1936, about the Old South, the Civil War, and Reconstruction, the movie was the largest and most expensive production in Hollywood up to that time, with a huge cast, massive sets (the city of Atlanta was burned down and then rebuilt), and hundreds of unshaven and bandaged extras trudging across the landscape." *NYer* I'm all for the serial comma (*q.v.*), but couldn't this sentence have been written with fewer than seven commas? *The New Yorker* has always been comma-happy; in the space of seven words, I recently saw five commas. One never sees so many commas in *The National Geographic, Smithsonian,* or *Scientific American.*

"It wasn't just that, as many people assume, higher gas prices functioned as a tax increase...." *NYer* The comma after "that" leads to confusion with sentences like, "It wasn't just that, but we had bad luck with the weather." **www** "As many people assume, it wasn't just that higher gas prices...."

The Old Let's-Chop-the-Sentence-Up-
To-Make-It-Seem-Profound Syndrome

"The reason for the decision to dissolve Prussia...lay in its association with the militaristic tendencies which had, in the eyes of the outside world, at least, launched Germany into two world wars." *NYR* **www** "tendencies which, in the eyes of the outside world at least, had launched...." (one less comma)

"The country has, in fact, become...." *NYR* **www** "The country, in fact, has become...."

"He understood perfectly well that horror and laughter could, under certain circumstances, be paired and reinforce each other...." *NYR* **www** "Under certain circumstances he understood...," or "that under certain circumstances, horror and laughter...." And, per the entry in Usage (*q.v.*), *one another* seems more appropriate, and more musical, than *each other.*

"The people standing patiently in line are not, it turns out, waiting to buy train tickets." *NYR* **www** "The people standing in line, it turns out, are not waiting...."

"He was, he told Goldman, joining a new trading company." *NYT* **www** "As he told Goldman, he was joining...."

"Poe was, surprisingly, much attached...." *NYer* **www** "Poe, surprisingly, was much attached...." (Later, the same nervous tic: "Poe was, nevertheless, desperate for....")

"Dyson has, as he admits, a restless nature...." *NYTM* **www** "As he admits, Dyson has..." or "Dyson admits that...."

"The five hundred people...supported a school where she received, from age six to twelve, the little formal education her circumstances allowed." *H* **www** "where, from age six to twelve, she received...."

"All that energy is also, of course, destructive...." *S* **www** "All that energy, of course, is also destructive...."

"Dennett was, it seems to me, apparently concentrating on...." *ACW* **www** "Dennett, it seems to me, was...."

"[The] administration's bailout plan generated enough anger that, Kruggel says, 'we realized....' " *N* **www** "generated enough anger, Kruggel says, that 'we realized....' "

"There is, incidentally, no crisis in...." *N* **www** "Incidentally, there is no crisis in...."

"But he, like other experts interviewed on Tuesday, was scratching his head...." *NYT* **www** "But like other experts interviewed on Tuesday, he was scratching his head...."

Simplify, simplify, simplify.

"Might" Makes Right

The past tense, in its conditional sense, of *may* is *might*. Why not use it, and be correct? "Mr. Fuller, who did not grow up in a culture-rich environment, may never have discovered his talent if...." *NYT* **www** "might never have discovered his talent...."

"She was, in fact, worried that she may be 15 pounds too heavy...." *WSJ* **www** "worried that she might be...."

"Chávez...has never really been able to accept the idea that Bolívar may have perished from natural causes...." *T* **www** "might have perished...."

"Rick Norsigian kept two boxes he bought at a yard sale...for four years before realizing they may be too valuable to store at home.... It would be two years before he realized they [sic] photos may be from Adams...." *CNN*

"Officials...did not say how long he may have been dead." *BH* In this case, "might" is not so good, because he was definitely dead. But "Officials did not say how long he *was* dead" is not so good, either; were the officials holding back information? Best is: "...they thought he had been dead."

The Mad Dash

Here are more examples of the needless use of the dash.

"The news wasn't good for Vergennes' beleaguered police department—Vergennes Chief of Police [name] was processed for driving a cruiser car while under the influence of prescription drugs." *EVT* **www** a colon, or two sentences?

"Trimming the flight controls also takes time—this relates only to the elevator in most basic training airplanes...." *FT*

"...Fokker turned the tables after examining the captured airplane—he engineered an interrupter gear allowing German pilots to fire between their propeller blades...." *FT* **www** with a colon or semicolon?

"Fleming, 17, compares the feeling of learning to fly with learning to drive—but better." *FT* (Note the somewhat skewed syntax.)

"Many of Yeats's greatest poems are written in ottava rima, an Italianate form that came into vogue with the Romantics—it was used by Shelley in 'The Witch of Atlas....' " *NYR* **www** "...the Romantics, for example by Shelley in..."?

"Humans can…conceive of how things could go wrong—including their own death…." *NS* (and please, *deaths*; see below)

"[The banks] printed their own money—$140 million in paper bills were in circulation by 1836." *NYer* **www** with a colon or semicolon?

"Hand scything is not common at ski areas—usually, massive machines and snowmakers groom and blast the mountainside…." *VL* **www** a period or semicolon?

"There's one constant in [this pilot's] career—change." *FT* God gave us colons: why use a dash instead?

"In time Galileo's findings began to trouble a powerful authority—the Catholic Church. *S* There had been earlier references to the Catholic Church; why set it off, here, with a dash?

I've picked on the magazine *Flight Training*, several times, in these quotes. To give credit where credit is due, the language insults are far fewer—and far less insulting—in *Flight Training* than in most highbrow literary magazines. Certified Flight Instructors and professional pilots make more innocent, therefore more forgivable, mistakes than do the people who write from the Land of the High Brows. Read any trade or hobby magazine, then compare it to your favorite "literary" magazine.

Excursus: Taking Pains

Regarding the need, in language, to take pains with detail, here is a quote from John Gardner, Secretary of Health, Education, and Welfare under President Lyndon Johnson:

"The society which scorns excellence in plumbing, because plumbing is a humble experience, and tolerates shoddiness in philosophy, because philosophy is an exalted activity, will have neither good plumbing nor good philosophy. Neither its pipes nor its theories will hold water."

If you think I'm petty and prickly, it's all right with me. The problem is, I am *not* petty and prickly, I just care that things be as good as they can be. Language is the liquid, the medium, in which I live, and it is a matter of concern to me that the liquid, the medium, not be noxious.

More from Hyphen Nation

In a magazine, I recently saw "Congressional" hyphenated *Congressio-nal*. Magazines must conserve space, of course, but wouldn't hyphenating between the *s*'s have produced a more visually pleasing result? I would rewrite an entire page before I would hyphenate the word, *Congressio-nal*. The British, by the way, are much more lax about hyphenation than us Americans (there's one for the Americans!), and often seem to hyphenate at random, with the maximization of type on the line being the only consideration.

"Swimming pool industry": hyphenate or not? I would say, not. A *swimming pool* is a very familiar entity.

"Homeland security issues": hyphenate or not? Again I would say, not. *Homeland security* is a single concept; its adjectival sense will be understood intuitively.

"Service": hyphenate based on the root (*serv-ice*), or on the sound (*ser-vice*)? I have dictionaries that recommend the former, and other dictionaries that recommend the latter. Language can be slippery, which is why we need lots of intellectual rosin.

The Death of Her Majesty's Royal Subject, The Subjunctive

One hears it all the time, especially from sports broadcasters: "If he would have been in position, that ball may not have gone into center field." **www** "If he *had been* in position...." *Would have*, in sentences like this one, is enough to make one's teeth tingle. And *might*, not *may*. (See above.)

Why are sports announcers hired who can't speak proper English? It's like hiring musicians who can't play very well. I'm not saying that every sports announcer has to speak the King's—or rather, the President's—English, only that if you are going to train a person to narrate games and read ads, you might as well listen to that person's pronunciation and syntax and, if necessary, encourage a little remedial English. Anyone who does anything well is not afraid of the word, "remedial." (I recently heard a commentator for an NBA basketball game pronounce the following sentence: "They went further than they thought." Another said, "I was originally born in Ohio." Where, I wonder, was he born after that?)

What's going to become of us when news broadcasters say, "The investigation is still continuing," something is "dwindling down," the Democrats need to be "convened together," he "retreated back" to his earlier position—or more than once refer to the "prostrate gland"?

Split Ends and Split Infinitives

A friend sent me a magazine article, recently, that nearly broke my heart. The article (from the magazine, *New Orleans*) was written in perfectly simple, clear, and direct prose; the punctuation was precise and unadorned. The article was a perfect (and beautiful) example of the kind of writing for which I am advocating. I drew two lessons from this article. 1) It *can* be done, that is, the kind of writing I am encouraging still exists; it is by no means impossible to achieve, or unreasonable to expect. 2) I am not a utopian. My modest standards *can* be met. I am not a person who insists, as a matter of principle, on being dissatisfied.

Now, there is no immutable law of the universe that says infinitives should not be split, and for the sake of clarity, sometimes they *must* be split. In the following examples, however, I think clarity would have been enhanced—and the writing would have been more graceful, and more musical—if they had *not* been split.

"[I]t's important to first become familiar with the airplane." *FT* **www** "[I]t's important, first, to become familiar with the airplane."

"How difficult is it to always be sorting out truth from lies...." **www** "How difficult is it always to be sorting out...." *D*

"She had to just trust the musicians...." *N* **www** "She had just to trust the musicians...."

"Bush administration officials are said to have repeatedly discouraged efforts...." *NYT* **www** "Bush administration officials are said repeatedly to have discouraged efforts...."

"If the team decides to not go with the casing...." *USA* **www** "not to go with...."

"It took a court clerk 40 minutes to simply read the list of 88 charges...." *NYT* Did the court clerk read the charges *simply*?

Excursus 2

Perhaps I should simply admit that the battle I am fighting has been lost. Language has gone on its way, its cheerful, sloppy way, and before long that sloppy language will perhaps be our new "correct" grammar. For the moment, however, I'm really put off by sentences like the following: "There is no owner's manual for the Oval Office, no school to learn how to be president." *NYT* **www** "no school *in which* to learn how to be president."

Brand New, Again

"A brand-new private pilot, I had logged approximately 80 hours...." *FT* Even though *brand new* is a descriptive phrase, this seems to me a case where the hyphen isn't necessary.

Whomakes Upthese Compoundwords?

anticoauthors
arenalike
backroom (as noun)
campuswide
canalside
collegebound
crabcake
decadelong
governmentwide
grenadelike
groundball
hyperaccessible
lowbudget
monthlong
policymakers
postcollapse
powerchords
preaccident
preseries
presstime
stadiumlike
timeslot

"A foolish consistency is the hobgoblin of little minds," said Ralph Waldo Emerson. On the other hand, it seems to me that *commonsense* consistency is a beautiful thing. At present, dictionaries are strangely inconsistent. Many of them list *boyfriend* (one word), but *girl friend* (two words). They list *backyard*, but no *frontyard*, *backseat*, but no *frontseat*, *backroom*, but no *frontroom*. I choose to be consistent, and write all such phrases as two words, with hyphens when necessary.

One proof that language evolves is in the way new words enter the dictionary. *Yearlong* has been around for a long time, but *daylong* and *weeklong* have only recently made the cut, and only in some dictionaries. Here's hoping that *monthlong*, *centurylong*, and *millenniumlong* will have to keep fighting, if not for a thousand years, at least for a hundred.

The hyphenation of prefixes is constantly in flux. For the present writer, the time is not yet right for *co-author* without a hyphen.

Locutions and Syntax from Outer Space

Of and *what*: why are *these* creeping into the language in usages like the following? "He's not as good *of* a hitter as *what* he used to be, which led the team to finish lower in the rankings than *what* it did last year." *Of* and *what* have absolutely no place in this sentence. **www** "He's not as good a hitter as he used to be, which led the team to finish lower in the rankings than it did last year." "He threw a pitch similar to what he threw last inning...." **www** "He threw a pitch similar to one he threw...."

"In the 1950s, John P.V. Heinmuller, a Longines Watch Company executive and an aviation enthusiast, donated 2,000 envelopes once transported by zeppelin to the Smithsonian...." *S* Did a zeppelin transport 2,000 envelopes to the Smithsonian?

"In some parts of the Midwest and Northeast, some streets are getting barely plowed." *NYT* Exactly *how* barely are they getting plowed?

"While much of the spilled oil in the Gulf has now been thankfully cleaned up...." *LT* What: *thank you, oil, for letting us clean you up? We cleaned you up thankfully?*

What a Little Moonlight—and the absence of a comma—Can Do: "As Soroush's words spread thanks to the Internet, Iran's grand ayatollahs entered the battlefield." *NYTM* Why did Soroush spread thanks to the Internet?

"Economists say India must invest heavily in transportation...but it is so far falling short." *NYT* It's too bad that it is falling short so very, very far.

"That is now all in question." *NYT* **www** "Now that is all in question."

"When asked their biggest complaint...." *BG* **www** "When asked what their biggest complaint was...." Oh copy editors, we hardly knew ye.

Who, That?

"[T]he trio of harmless country bumpkins that go camping with Brüno...." "[A] recently deceased pop star that has been in the news...." *NSWK* The writer used *that* and *who* correctly elsewhere in the article: why couldn't he have used them correctly here? As sloppy language seeps into common usage, and from there into dictionaries, the dictionaries effectively condone the original sloppiness. In some dictionaries, this is happening in the case of *who* and *that*. Properly, however, the relative pronoun, *who*, should be used with people, *that* with animals, places, and things. "The squirrel *that* was in the yard," but "The boy *who* brought me the newspaper."

If Only....

If only we could spruce up our language, at least *now and then*, by placing *only*, as an adverb, as close as possible to the thing it modifies....

"It helped that the Rays only could attract average crowds...." *BH* **www** "It helped that the Rays could attract only average crowds...."

"This is not true only in politics but...." *NYR* Clearly the sentence was meant to read, "This is true not only in politics, but...." Where was the copy editor?

"But Newton and his men only responded by gunning down yet another prominent Confederate." *ACW* **www** "responded only by gunning down yet another...."

"There will only be six shows...." *EVT* Couldn't it, more elegantly, have been, "There will be only six shows..."? Every now and then, hard as it is to believe, a writer uses *only* in a way that is both correct and pleasing to the ear: "To win sympathy and kudos...you have only to make clear how focused and intelligent you were...." *NYTM*

"Ortiz seemed to guess...swinging powerfully but connecting with only air." *NYT* "Connecting with *only air*"?

"Oakland starter Brett Anderson only allowed one earned run...." *MLB* **www** "allowed only one earned run...."

"The Yankee bullpen had another excellent day...marred by only Derek Jeter's throwing error...." *ESPN* **www** "marred only by." And the Yankee's pitching coach said (*MLB*), "Tonight was one of those days where we were up for the task." "*Tonight* was one of those *days*"? "Days *where*"? "Up *for* the task"?

Her and She, Again

"...I saw a young woman there but did not realize that it was her." *NYer* This is a classic case of "it was she" is correct, and "it was her" is not. And I would have inserted a comma after *there*. Newspaper editors (when they exist) seem to have forgotten that there *are* such things as commas.

To Each (Not) Their Own

"The *Smithsonian* online: Something for everyone, no matter how esoteric their interests." Better: "*her* [or *his*, or both] interests."

"He greets each one as if they were important...." *VL* Better: "as if *she* [or *he*] were important" (or rephrase sentence).

"[A]ny country that captures a pirate can seek to prosecute them." *NYDN* Better: "captures pirates," or "prosecute him or her."

In Terms of the Context

"Context is important." *S* So are time, snowmobiles, and broccoli. (See *context* in Usage)

Excursus 3

I keep finding notes to myself like the following:

I don't *like* being a nitpicker, a policeman, a schoolmarm, I just dislike being constantly tripped up by—and having to do double-takes over—language that is ambiguous and which requires two, if not more, readings before its sense emerges.

Some Things We Collectively Have More Than One Of

When many people have something, those somethings should be plural. Here is an example written correctly: "By the nineteen-seventies, after civil rights put an end to Jim Crow and the Great Migration stopped, six million people had left their homes." *NYer* Note that six million people did not leave their *home.* Why is it so difficult for writers to grasp this concept? Here are some examples written incorrectly, because *we, together,* have more than one of the things referred to.

Heads: "This isn't to say financial crises are all in our head...." *NYer*

Bodies: [after an assertion] "To which our smarty-pants body might reply...." *NYT*

Closets: "[The writer] can sound a bit puritanical when he scoffs at...the $600 worth of clothes in their closet that women supposedly haven't worn for a year." *N* It must be a *very* large closet.

Thermostats: "Why do we waste so much energy keeping our body thermostat...." *NS*

Laptops: "Now that everybody can check their...laptop for news...." *NYT*

Driver's licenses: "[A] bogus website asking motorists to register their vehicles and renew their driver's license using a credit card." *EVT* If motorists drive *vehicles,* don't they have driver's *licenses?*

Workplaces: "But we all have crosses to bear in our workplace." *ESPN*

Penises: Somewhere, recently (I didn't make a note of where), I saw, "Men should examine their penis...." No comment.

No Fun in "Fun"

"The hyperconsumption that was a fun spectator sport...." *N Fun?* **www** *enjoyable, pleasing, entertaining, amusing?*

Ellipses Need to Breathe, Too

At least ellipses (successions of dots to indicate omissions) beginning and ending sentences do: "I've managed to get along and do my duty, as I believe, and still save most of them....But...there are some cases where the law must be executed." *ACW* (The writer was Abraham Lincoln, though it was probably the transcriber who deleted the space before *But.*)

A New Stance Toward Reality

The five words, above, constituted a section heading in a recent copy of *The Nation.* Can one have a stance *toward* something? Wouldn't *A New Approach to*, or *Outlook on*, have been preferable? Or simply, *A New Reality?*

"While the doctrinal stance breaks no new ground, the question, like in March, is a matter of emphasis." *T doctrinal stance?* **www** *doctrine?* And *like in March* instead of *as in March* is inexcusable.

A Punctuation of Punctuation Follies

"All Vermont post offices will be open Friday, July 3, however, some will shorten retail lobby hours and close at noon." *EVT* Minimally needed to salvage this sentence is a semicolon after the 3.

"But, if we're going to start rewriting the Bible...." And three sentences later: "And, if Judas is let off the hook...." *NYer* Why the commas after *But* and *And?*

The exclamation point: when in doubt, leave it out. Just remember *Kiss: Keep It Simple, Stupid.*

83902238R00069

Made in the USA
San Bernardino, CA
01 August 2018